T4-ALD-522

THEORY AND PRACTICE
IN EDUCATIONAL ADMINISTRATION

EDUCATIONAL ADMINISTRATION
AND ORGANIZATION: IV
GENERAL EDITOR: **W. G. WALKER**

THEORY
AND PRACTICE
IN EDUCATIONAL
ADMINISTRATION

BY W. G. WALKER

PROFESSOR OF EDUCATION, UNIVERSITY OF NEW ENGLAND

CRANE, RUSSAK & COMPANY, INC.
52 Vanderbilt Avenue
New York, New York 10017

UNIVERSITY OF QUEENSLAND PRESS

© University of Queensland Press, St. Lucia, Queensland, 1970
Registered in Australia for transmission by post as a book
SBN 7022 0582 6
The text was set in Monotype Baskerville 11/12 and printed on
University Text 85 gsm
Printed and bound by Watson, Ferguson & Co., Brisbane
Designed by Cyrelle
Distributed by International Scholarly Book Services, Inc. Great Britain—
Europe — North America

73252

This book is copyright. Apart from any fair dealing for the purposes of
private study, research, criticism, or review, as permitted under the Copyright Act, no part may be reproduced by any process without written
permission. Enquiries should be made to the publishers.

BELMONT COLLEGE LIBRARY

PREFACE

This is very much a personal book. It is personal in the sense that it consists of a number of papers—all of which reflect a particular viewpoint on the administrative process—which have been read by the author to groups in centres as far apart as Perth, Western Australia; Palmerston North, New Zealand; Oxford, England; and Berkeley, California.

The papers were prepared for practitioners rather than professors and, although not arranged in chronological order, they reflect growth in the author's own particular approach to administration as an on-going process. Interested readers will readily discern the change in emphasis from administrative theory *per se* to administration as one aspect of organization theory; from a concern with teaching in the field to a growing interest in research; from an education-centred view of the study of administration to one heavily reliant upon concepts to be derived from the social sciences. There is, however, one assumption which has not changed over the five-year period represented by these papers—the need, in the interests of pupils no less than the teachers themselves, for maximum involvement of practitioners in the administration and organization of the educative enterprise—an assumption which accounts for the inclusion in this book of the teacher-centred papers on *The Fly Catchers* and *Obstacles to Freedom in the Schools*. It is with satisfaction, admittedly prejudiced, that the author sees the growing support for this assumption which emerges from the study of theorists like Presthus and Argyris and of researchers like Gross and Herriot and Likert and Seashore.

The book is at least as much concerned with the "is's" of administration as with the "ought's". The view is taken that in the field of administration as in the field of teaching or in any profession, successful practice is dependent as much upon science as upon art for its guidelines. Thus the achievement of the "ought's" depends markedly upon the insights which a study of the "is's" reveals.

Nearly all the papers which make up this book have already been printed elsewhere. Indeed, it has been the constant demand for copies of these contributions which has persuaded the author that they should be presented in book form.

The period covered by the papers (roughly 1962-68) coincides with the development in Australia of an extraordinary interest in the theory and practice of educational administration. During these five years several universities have introduced or strengthened their offerings in the field, and far-sighted senior administrators in government school systems and independent schools have encouraged principals, inspectors, supervisors, and others in executive positions to take advantage of such offerings. Some Departments of Education have gone so far as to introduce their own courses in the area; others are planning to do so.

A number of well-known Australian educators have been associated with these developments, but it would be impossible to describe their contributions in this preface. However, since this is a "personal" book, the author wishes to acknowledge his particular debt to his colleagues at the University of New England. This University has played a major role in the development of the study of educational administration in Australia—notably in the early stages through the innovative capacity of a few members of staff of the Armidale Teachers' College, which enjoys a special relationship with the University. Dr. G. W. Bassett, now Professor and Dean of the Faculty of Education at the University of Queensland, and Mr. A. R. Crane, now Principal of the Armidale Teachers' College, were largely responsible for persuading the University to introduce in 1959 postgraduate studies in the field: the next Principal of the College, Mr. G. W. Muir (now New South Wales Director of Teacher Education) supported and encouraged this development in association with Professor J. A. Richardson, who was appointed to the Foundation Chair of Education at the University of New England in 1961. Professor Richardson is now Foundation Professor of Education at the Flinders University of South Australia.

Since 1959 the present author has shared with his colleagues the privilege of planning and executing the University's postgraduate offerings in educational administration, latterly as foundation editor of the *Journal of Educational Administration*.

The papers reproduced in this volume are, in one sense at least, historical documents, for they represent, for many of the organizations which invited them, their first contact with the notion of educational administration as a proper field of academic study, based upon theoretical concepts to be understood, a body of knowledge to be studied and researched, a practice to be mastered.

Few authors can look back over a paper delivered four or five years earlier without recoiling in horror from statements which appear in retrospect naive, if not just plain stupid. This author is no exception, but he has judged it proper to reproduce the papers largely as they first saw the light of day, the only emendations being the removal of some sections which are blatantly overlapping or repetitive. Certain sections necessarily remain repetitive, since omission of key concepts and references would emasculate the arguments presented in particular chapters. The papers are therefore, without apology, printed essentially in their original form—as papers to be read *to* administrators rather than to be read *by* them.

Several of the papers have book lists appended. Hopefully, readers will find the perusal of those books, like the papers reproduced here, as challenging an exercise as the author found the preparation of these chapters.

W. G. WALKER,
Armidale, 1968

CONTENTS

ONE

THE CHALLENGE OF EDUCATIONAL ADMINISTRATION

Adapted from papers read at the Australian College of Education Seminar on Educational Administration, University of Western Australia, Perth, January 1965 and at a meeting of the Palmerston North Institute of Educational Research, University of Manawatu, New Zealand, November 1965.

INTRODUCTION

It was Mark Twain who claimed that there were only three certainties in this life—death, taxes, and rain on the Fourth of July holiday. Obviously Mark Twain had little to do with schools for had he had such experience he would have added a fourth certainty: that sooner or later somebody would be asked at a conference of principals to deliver an address containing the word "challenge" in the title!

The topic as stated is far too broad for the immediate interests of this conference, which, I understand, was arranged chiefly to meet the interests of school administrators. I have taken it upon myself therefore, to avoid discussion of the administration of universities and other tertiary institutions and to omit reference to implications at state and national levels. This does not mean that much of what I have to say is irrelevant to these areas of administration; nor does it mean that they should be avoided in discussion. However, the challenges facing educational administration in the schools alone are legion. They are challenges which have implications not only for your child and mine, but also for our national prosperity and, indeed, survival, for the most efficient and economic expenditure of our tax dollar, for skill and flexibility in decision making, and for meeting the effects of rapid social change. I have discussed some of these challenges in publications elsewhere,[1] while others are too complicated to warrant discussion here. In short, I have interpreted my remit to include the raising of issues, the suggesting of books and papers for your reference and the questioning, perhaps, of some cherished assumptions.

I intend to approach my task by discussing a small number of challenges *seriatim*. These individual challenges overlap at several points but the arrangement should simplify discussion. I hope to show that there are several dragons in the path of the Australian school administrator, none of which is more fearsome and yet so deserving of conquest as the dragon of "common sense" on whose scaly sides may be clearly discerned the slogan "anti-science".

With some shame I must confess that to a very large extent I, like most other educators, have been forced to sign a treaty with this monster. From time to time in these papers I shall express ideas which are merely opinion, which cannot be supported by scientific evidence, which seem to be "common sense" and which may well in future years, if not immediately, be demonstrated to be quite wrong. I make no pretensions to be a latter day St. George; yet now and again, I shall twist the tail of "anti-science" and you may feel him wince and hear him roar with anger at approximately the same time as you, perhaps, experience similar reactions.

SOME DEFINITIONS

Perhaps two terms need to be defined. These are simple, everyday terms, but I think their use should be established *before* we proceed, for everyday terms like "organization" and "administration" have a habit of meaning different things every day.

I have selected my definitions from Ordway Tead's well-known book, *The Art of Administration*. He writes:

> An organization is a combination of the necessary human beings, equipment, facilities, and appurtenances, materials and tools, assembled in some systematic and effective co-ordination in order to accomplish some desired and defined objective.[2]

[2]

At this stage I want to do no more than to draw your attention to the words "systematic", "co-ordination" and "desired and defined objective". Administration he defines as

> the process and agency which is responsible for the determination of the aims for which an organization and its management are to strive, which establishes the broad policies under which they are to operate and which gives general oversight to the continuing effectiveness of the total operation in reaching the objectives sought.[3]

Thus, administration not only defines the purposes of the organization but contributes to their achievement. It is a *service* process. It is essential to the existence and survival of an organization, but it needs to be seen in proper perspective. *Administration does not exist to further administration*. It is important, in view of what I am to say later on, to link with this definition Tead's view of the administrator as an educator of those for whom he is responsible. As he puts it, "The sound maxim is to make every administrative contact one which helps to advance the learning, the understanding and the concurrence of those being dealt with".[4]

THE CHALLENGES

Let us now move to the challenges and discuss each one briefly. The Challenges I shall discuss are those of, respectively, purpose, professionalism, isolation, size, and science.

The challenge of purpose

This challenge is the key to all others. If we cannot state clearly just what it is we are aiming for, we are in a sorry state indeed. Yet my researches and those of others suggest that many of us are in such a state.

One of the major challenges of administration is that aims or purposes fit into two distinct compartments. The school administrator, for example, must have in mind firstly the aims of one interaction process which we call teaching and secondly of another interaction process which we call administration. Putting this in another way he is concerned not only with the

[3]

aim of organizational achievement, but with the aim of organization maintenance, for success in the former is largely dependent upon success in the latter. It is the former which should be of prime concern to the administrator, for having spelt it out he has a guide for his actions in regard to the latter.

Many, perhaps most, of us would be considerably embarrassed if asked to stand now and state lucidly and truthfully just what we are trying to achieve. Do we really seek to develop character or is it rather to achieve examination success? Are we really seeking to imbue a living philosophy of education or rather to persuade the Department that we are worthy of promotion? Are we really trying to meet the needs of each individual child, or are we merely steering a pleasant avoid-trouble-at-all-costs course like that acrobatic principal who sat on the fence with one ear close to the ground so that he could ascertain which way the wind was blowing?

It may be objected that it is unfair to ask principals to state clearly the purposes or goals of their institutions, for education is, after all, a many-sided process. This may well be so, but it is notable that when headmasters or teachers are picked out from the ordinary for special compliment or condemnation, particular instances of achievement or lack of achievement are almost invariably cited.

I would be the first to agree that aims are far from simple to state, but would also be the first to assert that an institution which has not consciously made an effort to state its aims in terms which are meaningful, even if not easily measurable, to individual children and individual teachers hardly deserves the description of a "good school".

Without such a clear and accepted statement of aim, how can maximum staff involvement, as distinct from staff *direction*, be assured? How can the high-sounding phrases of the syllabus be converted into goals for action? How can achievement be measured or success and failure judged?

Education and its service process, educational administration, has, through the centuries, been so weighed down by cant and humbug that to this day, as Hemphill puts it, we refer to it in "homely parables and analogies".[5] Simon points out that we talk about organization in terms not unlike those used by a Ubangi Medicine Man to discuss disease.[6]

What, for example, do we mean by an "efficient" school? How does one measure inputs and outputs in education— moral, social, intellectual, and so on? We certainly claim to do so, for children pass or fail exams each year, and teachers are promoted or occasionally demoted each year, apparently on the basis of some criteria which are based on purposes.

I have my own particular prejudice for a statement of the aim of educational administration. It is the one presented by the author of that classic objective study of centralization and decentralization, Francois Cillié: "The complete liberation of the potentialities of the individual pupil and the individual teacher".[7]

I am also prejudiced in the belief that this statement of aim can be expressed in meaningful and even roughly measurable terms by a staff and head of good faith, though I do not for a moment consider that the terms will be identical in schools A and B.

Less prejudiced, and certainly more reliant upon experimental evidence, is my belief that group behaviour is goal-centred, that the human being likes to find satisfaction in his work group and that teachers who are involved in the definition and evaluation of their task are more likely to contribute to the liberation of the potentialities of individual children.

The achievement of an aim like this, which clearly seeks to release the potential of teachers through group and individual involvement, assumes a quality of leadership which is not automatically granted to one assigned the official status of principal. It demands a type of leadership which makes authority effective.

For the present I shall content myself with pointing out that in recent years there has been a great deal of research carried out on the behaviour of leaders, notably by workers at Ohio State University. One of the most interesting findings of this research has been the isolation of two key dimensions of leader behaviour: Initiating Structure-in-Interaction (the formal organization dimension) and Consideration (the human relations dimension).

The aims of organization maintenance are clearly achieved through the recognition of the existence of dimensions like these. The achievement of high morale, adequate co-ordination, and effective communication, for example, are at least in part dependent upon the statement of aims in words which have clear meaning, which can be expressed in behavioural terms, and which can be measured in some way. How else can the effectiveness of administration be assessed? What is administrator accomplishment if not organizational change produced as a result of his behaviour?[8]

The challenge of professionalism

A few lines above I asserted that there is considerable evidence from research to support my faith in staff involvement as a means of achieving organizational goals and organizational maintenance.

I regret that I cannot produce such evidence to support my next contention that there is a case for the professionalization of administration. All I can do is to rely on the arguments of example and analogy.

It may surprise some of you to learn that membership in the American Association of School Administrators is now limited to applicants who have completed two years postgraduate work in educational administration at an accredited university. Of course, this does not mean that all, or even most, American school administrators have professional qualifications, but it does mean that in one country at least some form of professional pre-service or in-service education in educational administration is being taken very seriously indeed.

For nearly half a century there has been a growing conviction in the United States that administration is not a task for an amateur. The traditional British and Australian approach has been "Mr. X is a good teacher—indeed, our best teacher. He is too good to remain a teacher. We'll make him an administrator".

This practice is well-known to us in Australia today. If a man is to be a teacher we train him to be a teacher; if an engineer, we train him to be an engineer; if a naval officer, we train him to be a naval officer. But if a man is to be a school principal, do we train him to be a school principal? Of course, we do not, unless we wish to delude ourselves by referring to several years of class teaching which may or may not provide some vicarious experiences in administration as "training".

The suggestion that specific training can be given for budding school administrators is still regarded as heresy in some circles, especially in that great stronghold of amateurism, Great Britain, and, let us face it, in another declining stronghold of amateurism, in the Antipodes.

What puzzles some of us is the question why *educational* administration is singled out for amateur status when in so many other fields of endeavour the training of administrators is much more generally taken for granted. Each state has its Institute of Management dedicated to the improvement of management in business, several universities offer undergraduate and postgraduate courses in public administration and business administration. Anyone interested in the administration of banks, the army, hospitals, government departments or even hotels will find courses being offered in one or more technical colleges, universities or some other specialised institution somewhere in Australia, as Cunningham and Radford's book, *Training the Administrator*, makes quite clear.[9]

Irrespective of our personal attitude towards amateurism, we must face the fact that it seems to be dying a lingering death in nearly every field of administration, including at last the administration of educational institutions. Courses in educational administration have been introduced or are planned in nearly every state of Australia. It is now, or soon will be, possible for a student to study educational administration at one or more levels at the Universities of Sydney, Queensland, Monash, Western Australia, and New England, and from this year onwards at the Perth Technical College. Few of the courses offered are as yet sufficiently disciplined and challenging to be described as providing full professional preparation, but some of them are moving towards such a standard.

The point we have reached in the argument is this: the liberation of the potentialities of the individual child is the task for which the individual teacher is trained. The task of co-ordinating an organization in order to permit this educative relationship to develop to its fullest is the task for which the individual administrator *should* be trained.

In a recent publication, Jenson and Clark[10] point out that

> Minimal characteristics of a profession include a definite specialized body of knowledge and skills, a prescribed pre-service preparation program, legal sanction for practitioners, an ethical code and a system of self policing by members in the profession.

In the United States at least some school administrators are well on their way to professional status as measured against these criteria, and I would not be surprised if the same were true in Australia within two or three decades.

I shall discuss some aspects of this development in a later paper, but for the moment I wish to stress that there is coming into existence a specialized body of knowledge and skills about administration *qua* administration which any budding administrator worth his salt will want to master. Having mastered it, however, he is presented with yet another challenge, this time arising from his professionalism: that of ensuring that as a school administrator *he keeps his eye firmly on the individual child* and is not blinded by the administrivia of tuckshops, buses, and bookrooms. In some places in the United States there have been employed otherwise excellent administrators who appear to have little appreciation of the school's mission, but who nonetheless, as members of a managerial élite, receive higher salaries and greater social esteem than do the teachers they employ. Is such a state of affairs unavoidable?

The challenge of isolation

The next challenge—that of isolation—is closely linked with the preceding challenge of professionalization. One of the criteria listed by Jenson and Clarke suggests that the development of a profession is apparently dependent upon public acceptance of the fact that the practitioner possesses an expertise which has its roots in esoteric knowledge mastered by members of his calling.[11]

[8]

It is obvious that as yet most Australian educational administrators cannot claim such expertise. It is equally obvious that such expertise is rapidly developing as administrators enrol in university courses and rub shoulders with students of administration in related disciplines and with interstate and even international colleagues. But such men and women are still rarities. Australian administrators of public schools have traditionally lived in a tight little world more or less defined by the state system in which they practise. Very few have had experience, either as teachers or administrators, in the systems of other states or other countries. Even fewer have had some experience in the Catholic or independent schools which constitute the other two Australian so-called "systems".

Each system constitutes what amounts to something approaching a closed shop. The state system, for example, trains and employs its own teachers and promotes many of them to administrative positions. Incredibly, the more senior the person the more difficult it is to transfer from one state system to another and the more difficult it is to obtain exchange positions with other states and other countries.

The result is that each state develops a kind of educational establishment, as inbred in some ways as the establishment attacked by Professor Francis Anderson in his epoch-making address in Sydney during 1901. Principals, though not directly members of the establishment, do aspire to membership and cut their cloth accordingly. And in view of their restricted experiences, who can blame them?

To be sure, there are signs of greater intercourse of ideas among schoolmen. Organizations like the Australian College of Education and the New Education Fellowship have brought together at least some members of the establishments of each of the three systems throughout Australia. But we would be deluding ourselves if we argued that these organizations represented any more than a small proportion of school principals in each state.

It is also true that there is more interstate and international movement among departmental officers of the rank of superintendent (or inspector) and above than ever before. However,

[9]

I am sure that a week's conference in Melbourne or even three days at the University of California are poor substitutes for actual experience working in another system.

It should be rewarding to think through the principles which appear to underlie our apparent desire to discourage interstate or international exchange of principals. Perhaps it is alleged to be of some advantage to teachers or to the Education Departments. Certainly, it cannot have been adopted with the interests of children or of society at large in mind.

So far we have talked about the isolation of principals from their fellows in other systems, other states, and other countries. There is another form of isolation, however, which is even more remarkable. This is the isolation of school administrators from administrators in other fields. Australian technical colleges, which for years have attracted administrators from business, industry, hospitals, and the public service, have rarely attracted an administrator from a school. Few schoolmen choose to include a course in public administration in their first or second degree structure. I know nothing about the membership of the Western Australian Branch of the Australian Institute of Management, but I will hypothesize with some certainty that it contains very few, if any, educational administrators in its ranks. I do know that at a recent date only one headmaster had attended the Australian Administrative Staff College at Mt. Eliza, and then only through the generosity of an industrial enterprise.

The schoolman worth his salt should always be on the lookout for ways and means of releasing the full potential of every child and of every teacher. It does not matter whether these ideas come from a Catholic or Lutheran school, or whether they were gleaned in a factory in Melbourne or an institute in Manchester. The important thing is the *idea*.

Isolation can be overcome by wide reading, attendance at conferences, travel, membership of organizations, university courses, and by experience in other positions. This broadening of the bases of our knowledge and the task of keeping up to date in our profession is a challenge indeed.

The challenge of size

It is perhaps at first sight contradictory that I should speak in one breath of the challenge of isolation and in the next of the challenge of size.

I do not intend in this paper to devote much time to size as it relates to the state education departments. I will merely content myself by pointing out that to an extent not commonly observed in other school systems, Australian public schools are closely associated with the large, rather impersonal bureaucracies which constitute the state education departments. For this reason alone I feel justified in drawing attention to what Dimock[12] describes as "the law of diminishing managerial returns" and to a quotation from Kandel which probably is still pretty close in some states to the nub of a situation which he described in 1938:

> What comes to count for most is the "system". Education under such conditions ceases to be dependent upon the release of the capacities and insight of trained personalities and becomes formal and mechanized ... Uniformity and a certain monotony rather than variety and flexibility become the characteristics of such a system.[13]

I would very much like to stray along the fascinating highways and by-ways of centralization and decentralization and to discuss their effects on individual schools, but shall resist the temptation, as the challenge of *school* size is of more immediate interest to us. I know of no community which is more likely to be truly educative in the sense of the liberation of individual potentialities than the small one-teacher school with its pleasant teacher-pupil relationships, individual instruction, unhurried tempo, and busy working spirit. Such schools are rapidly becoming novelties in some parts of Australia, as are the virtues which marked them as educational powerhouses. Schools have become so large that they must be "administered", but, as I have tried to suggest on a number of occasions in the course of this paper, the proper task of the contemporary administrator

[11]

is to preserve the above "small school" virtues in the large school for which he is responsible.

Size brings with it a number of advantages, notably economy in the deployment of staff and in the provision of buildings and services. It can also produce some problems. For example, it usually produces departmentalization and specialization. For a moment or two let us consider some of the anti-educational effects of this, as suggested by some recent work I have been doing in Australian high schools. Teachers tend to regard themselves as teachers of subjects rather than as teachers of children. Liaison among the several departments becomes awkward or even non-existent. Communication with the principal becomes difficult to achieve. All of this is not to say that size *must* produce these problems; merely that they are usually produced and must be guarded against.

There is not time or space to pursue this subject further. Let us be content to quote from a recent pioneering study by Barker and Gump: *Big School, Small School. Inter alia* the authors conclude:

> The large school has authority: its grand exterior dimensions, its long halls and myriad rooms, and its tides of students all carry an implication of power and rightness. The small school lacks such certainty: its modest building, its short halls and few rooms, and its students, who move more in trickles than in tides, give an impression of a casual or not quite decisive educational environment.
>
> These are outside views. They are illusions. Inside views reveal forces at work stimulating and compelling students to more active and responsible contributions to the enterprises of small than of large schools . . .
>
> Common-sense theories about schools are not adequate bases for policy decisions . . . The educational process is a subtle and delicate one about which we know little, but it surely thrives on participation, enthusiasm and responsibility. Our findings and our theory posit a negative relationship between school size and individual student participation . . . What size should a school be? . . . A school should be small enough that students are not redundant.[14]

The challenge of science

The work of Barker and Gump with its scientific testing of predictions based on theory provides an excellent example of the scientific movement in educational administration.

Basic to the development of any science, whether it be a physical science like nuclear physics or a behavioural science like those upon which administration is based, is the development of theory.

In another place[15] I have presented a number of arguments based largely on the writings of Professor D. E. Griffiths of New York University, pertinent to the place of theory in educational administration. A resume of the argument is as follows:

The almost universally accepted dichotomy between theory and practice is founded on the untenable assumption that it is possible to make decisions and take actions quite independently of our motives. Our behaviour invariably serves the pursuit of some goal and our motives are shaped by certain explicit and implicit theories which we hold. Any attempt at making a decision takes place in a supporting conceptual framework.

All of us theorize, but few of us develop *good* theory, i.e. theory which reveals uniformities in the subject matter of the theory, which enables us to predict precisely in accordance with established criteria and which provides guides to action. A good theory thus has potential for (*a*) explaining and predicting events, and (*b*) the production of new knowledge.

An essential correlate of theory construction is concept development. A concept is simply a term to which a particular meaning has been attached. Once the meaning has been attached to the term, the term should always be used with that particular meaning.

Another important characteristic of a theory is that even in the physical sciences important factors may be left out in its formulation. Hence a theory may be the truth, but not the whole truth. It should be evaluated on the basis of what is in, rather than what is left out. Further, no one theory is likely to be *the* theory. Metatheory applicable to educational organizations is most unlikely of achievement at this stage of our development.

Again, there is nothing to be gained from being afraid of theory. A theory can be wrong and still lead to progress. Explicit theory—even *wrong* explicit theory—is better than implicit theory or no theory at all.

The uses of theory are *a*) as a guide to new knowledge and *b*) as a guide to action. With regard to *a*) Dallenbach[16] writes: "Doing something without a theory is not a scientific experiment. It is mere busy work."[16] With regard to *b*) Getzels' concept of theory as a relational map (not as an itinerary) is pertinent: "Theories without practices, like maps without routes, may be empty, but practices without theories, like routes without maps, are blind."[17]

Although there are some promising theories available to both researchers and practitioners in educational administration, the general level of research and practice is no higher than that achieved by chemists before the discovery of the periodic system. Educational administration may be described as being in an age of educational alchemy.

Are we content in the thermo-nuclear age to rely upon alchemy for our professional insights? Are we to continue to rely upon "hunches", experience, the evidence gleaned from the certitude of myths and legends? Can we afford not to turn to the social scientist for the development of theory and testing of concepts relevant to our practice?

During the latter years of the nineteenth century a fresh breeze began to blow through the folklore which was then called medicine. Describing the trauma which the Johns Hopkins medical school suffered at that time, Professor George Miller comments:

> The unhappy truth is that for more than a century most professors of medicine were ... practitioners who taught almost exclusively by telling students about things they believed to be true on the basis of personal experience or folklore alone ... It was clearly necessary to find a new kind of professor, one prepared to devote a major portion of his energies to academic pursuits, to bring to the care of patients

in this protected setting a spirit of enquiry which would allow disease to be studied systematically and the data derived from such study shared widely.[18]

Perhaps in our own field one of the greatest challenges facing us (assuming that we regard the liberation of the potentialities of children as having an importance equal to the curing of disease) is to prepare ourselves for just such a fresh breeze in our thinking about the study of educational administration.

TWO

PROBLEMS OF SCHOOL ORGANIZATION

Adapted from papers read at the Australian College of Education Seminar on Educational Administration, University of Western Australia, Perth, January 1965 and at the triennial conference of the Headmistressses of the Independent Girls' Schools of Australia, Adelaide, August 1964.

INTRODUCTION

A year or two ago one of my students presented me with a well-thumbed volume entitled *A Handbook of School Management* written by Mr. P. W. Joyce, A.M.T.C.D., M.R.I.A.,[1] Headmaster of the Central Model Schools, Dublin and published in 1867.

How I wish that I could solve the problems of school organization with the confidence reflected in Mr. Joyce's Chapter 2, "Systems of Organization":

> Visit any national school, the teacher of which has not adopted a proper system of organization, and with great probability you will observe the business carried on in something like the following manner. One or two classes are standing up, receiving instruction from the master and a monitor; all the rest of the pupils are sitting, either in desks or in forms round the walls of the room, some few of the more advanced writing or working from their arithmetics, a few others preparing lessons with apparent attention, but the great majority, especially of the young children, openly idle . . . Let us then begin by laying down this important maxim, which may be called "The principle of perpetual employment":—Every child in the school should be engaged at some useful employment, at every moment during the entire day.[2]

Mr. Joyce knows how to handle this situation and he provides the reader with the choice of three sure-fire solutions, each

[16]

described in minute detail. The Bipartite System, for example, requires children to stand on semicircles while learning from their monitors. We are left in no doubt about these semicircles:

> Suppose AB to be a portion of the school wall. Take a point O for the centre, about 15 or 18 inches from the wall, and with a radius of three feet, describe the semicircle CDE and continue the ends to the wall by the perpendiculars CF and EG. The circle so marked, which may be regarded as of moderate size, will hold twelve pupils . . . The circles ought to be placed as far apart as the draft space will allow, as this tends greatly to lessen noise; but the distance between two adjacent circles should never be less than two feet.[3]

Mr. Joyce has a good excuse for his pedantic approach to school organization. He writes for pupil-teachers and those who have no training whatsoever. He writes for the Ireland of the 1860's and his book is a perfect example of Getzels' "itinerary" approach.[4] I am, of course, much more interested in Getzels' "relational maps" than in his "itineraries".

I intend in this paper to speak generally about organizations and to describe briefly some of the characteristics of organizations which are well known to scholars in the field. At the end of the paper I shall raise some particular issues for further consideration.

ADMINISTRATIVE ORGANIZATION

In my earlier paper I gave you Ordway Tead's[5] definition of organization. By now you will realize that we cannot conceive of administration without organization. As we have seen, administration is indeed the process which sets the organization's aims, and through co-ordination, seeks their achievement. Thus it is through organization that administration must act. It is hardly necessary for me to point out that poor organization leads to dissipated effort, wasted resources, and poor results.

Organization has been defined in a number of ways. Some people emphasize its formal or legal structure, others the human relationships involved. There is general agreement, however, that an organization consists of a number of people, hierarchically ordered and joined together for the achievement of a common purpose. Clearly, a school, like a factory or a bank, is an organization. Such organization may consist of two people, two hundred, or two thousand.

What are some of the features of organizations like schools? Firstly, there is a job to be done—educating children. Secondly, there is a division of labour which requires a co-ordination of the specialized activities of the members of the group. Thirdly, there is an additional element, or congeries of elements, which with interaction lends the organization its dynamic quality. These are the "human" elements—the motivations, expectations, attitudes and so on of the members of the organization.

Administration is necessary in order that these combined elements may be maintained in what Cornell[6] describes as a "zone of rationality" or Lonsdale[7] as a "dynamic equilibrium". Administration defines general and specific purposes, and co-ordinates the activities of the organization in seeking those purposes. Administration, then, cannot be conceived of as merely managing an organization. It is an integral part of it.

We have agreed that the chief aim of school administration is the liberation of the maximum potentialities of the individual pupil and the individual teacher. We have also agreed that the aims of education are achieved through the efforts of individual teachers interacting with individual children and that this relationship is at its best when the teacher feels free to adapt his teaching to the individual's peculiar interests and needs.

We well know, however, that for the overwhelming majority of individual teachers and individual pupils this relationship must take place within an organization which we call "school", consisting of several hundred or even several thousand other individuals.

It is also well known that as institutions grow in size they become more formalized and that it becomes increasingly difficult to ensure or even to encourage the type of freedom which this individual interaction seems to demand. As Cornell has put it so well,

> The more formal the organization the more predetermined the lines of interaction are inclined to be, the more relationships are inclined to be guided by the defined role rather than the individual personality.[8]

He points out that formal structure in its extreme form is bureaucracy, a type of organization found in both government and non-government institutions. He argues that while administration should be viewed from the standpoint of the organization as a whole, and thus has an integrating function, it also has an important centrifugal function:

> A team operating in symphony toward the achievement of an organizational goal must have correct decisions regarding purposes and means of achieving these purposes, and what is more, an understanding of and an acceptance by all members of the team of the same decision.[9]

This leads us to the concept of efficiency in the consideration of organization *per se*. Organization takes away some of the autonomy of the individual. In compensation for this he must receive certain satisfactions. An organization may, in this sense, be described as efficient to the extent that it offers a surplus of inducements to its members to co-operate. If the motivations of the individuals concerned and the objectives of the organization are in harmony, then the personal contribution of effort in the co-operative system is maintained and the system is an organization which is said to be efficient.

Cornell's criticism of the undue emphasis on predetermined lines of interaction is not an argument against organization. It is, however, an argument for careful planning in organization. Dewey described the problem in enlightened terms when he wrote,

> It is reasonably obvious that organization may become a hindrance to freedom; it does not take us far to say that the trouble lies not in organization but in one organization. At the same time it must be admitted that there is no effective or objective freedom without organization.[10]

So we are faced with the following situation: we wish to encourage individuality and freedom on the part of teachers and children; at the same time we cannot give them unlimited freedom, for that way lies anarchy. Yet if we step too far in the other direction—perhaps unconsciously (for the influence of bureaucracy can be pernicious)—we may readily rob the school of that vitality and adaptability on which education thrives.

We agreed earlier that organization aims at co-ordination, or control. One of the great problems in organization is that unskilled administrators are rarely aware of the real patterns of power and communication within their own systems. As a result they fail to keep their fingers on the pulse of the organization and their most central function, that of decision making, suffers from lack of understanding and lack of information. Culbertson and others have claimed that the most important aspects of the administrative process are decision making, communication, morale-building, and initiating change.[11]

Let us discuss some further facets of organization and attempt from time to time to relate them to Culbertson's key aspects.

FORMAL AND INFORMAL ORGANIZATIONS

Most of you will be only too well aware that organization is typified by both a formal structure and an informal structure.

The formal organization is the one which looks so impressive when we draw our organization chart. The chart shows clearly the official lines of authority, the functional units of the organization, the responsibilities of the different units and the established channels of communication.

I discussed this point at a conference of headmistresses of independent schools in Adelaide and I am sure they will not object if I reproduce for you an organization chart I obtained for their use. The chart, that of St. Agatha's, a typical girls' independent school, looks something like this:

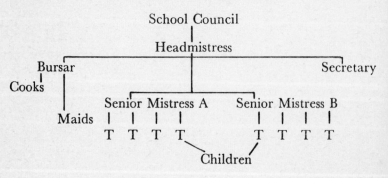

The headmistress of St. Agatha's Academy (incidentally, St. Agatha's is not in Western Australia, nor will you find it listed in any Australian schools directory) is very proud of this chart. It is so neat, so tidy, so easy to understand.

However, I happen to know that it is also almost meaningless. For example, the chart shows "line" and "staff" personnel as though the "staff" who have a service function have no *power* by virtue of their positions.

At St. Agatha's the Bursar, who has been at the school for thirty years, has a very strong influence over the headmistress, a comparative newcomer of five years' vintage. When the staff came to the headmistress with a proposal to implement a textbook hire scheme, *he* was the one who influenced her to reject the scheme; when a new school hospital was mooted, *he* was the one who convinced the headmistress that it was not required. Yet the bursar is shown on the chart as being a service officer who serves and assists the principal!

Further, although the headmistress is official "leader" of the school, one of the senior mistresses is openly recognized by most teachers as their official spokesman and guardian. In times of stress they turn to her, not to the headmistress, who has repeatedly demonstrated her ineptness in handling such situations.

Obviously, St. Agatha's, like any other organization, has an informal organization which has developed as a structure of personalities rather than of authority or function. In this particular school the only person with authority to give the secretary work to type is the principal. In fact, the whole staff knows that Senior Mistress B can get work done by the secretary a good deal more quickly than can the headmistress.

There is nothing unusual about this. As Barnard points out,

> Informal organizations are found within all formal organizations, the latter being essential to order and consistency, the former to vitality. There are mutually reactive phases of co-operation, and they are mutually dependent.[12]

The informal organization is of importance, however, not merely because it establishes the customs, mores, and norms of the organization, but because, being free of the rigidity of the

[21]

formal structure, it creates conditions under which new invention, new discovery and new practices may develop.

The immediate relevance of all this to administration is that successful decision making, communicating, morale building, and initiation of change are unlikely to eventuate unless the principal is aware of the dynamics of *both* structures, formal and informal.

FORMAL AND INFORMAL COMMUNICATION

This awareness is closely linked to the process of communication. It is axiomatic that no organization can exist without communication. Within any institution there are formal and informal communication "nets".

Listening to a group of principals talking, one could be excused for assuming that the only form of communication known to them flows downwards—the principal issues his instructions, which are then passed "down the line". One of the most common mistakes made by administrators is ignoring the existence of communication in other directions. Horizontal communication, for example, must take place between the two senior mistresses when they are interpreting an instruction from above for application in their houses. Is there no significance in the informal problem solving which goes on every evening in the mistresses' common room at St. Agatha's?

By far the most important aspect of communication for administrators, however, is upward communication. This is the channel through which the principal receives feedback and is provided with information which he can use to assess the effectiveness of his downward communication. Lonsdale puts it very well:

> Feedback is the process through which an organization learns: it is the input from the environment to the system telling it how it is doing as a result of its output to the environment. This feedback–input is then used to steer the operation of the system.[13]

While every aspect of communication should be of concern to the principal, it is upward communication which is most

commonly blocked. This typically happens at the level immediately below that of principal. I have often noticed that in
schools with deputy principals much information does not reach
the principal, who continues on his happy way, sitting pre-
cariously but innocently on a hotbed of trouble. The reasons
for this blockage are not always easy to find, but common cases
are: a) the deputy tries to protect the head from complaints or
other overt symptoms which he considers are too trifling to
concern the busy "boss"; and b) the deputy seeks to prevent
the head from hearing information that might reflect adversely
on his (the deputy's) own administration.

Where there is no deputy, senior teachers are likely to block
communication in a similar way. Of course, these controls may
well be exercised subconsciously, but this does not detract from
the fact that they do exist.

The whole question of communication is closely allied to the
social structure of the school. When we administer, we interact
with people, whether we run a school, a church, or a hotel.
These people seek to earn a living, to find satisfaction, to experience success, and to find affection, irrespective of their profession or status.

One of the ways in which they seek to achieve these ends is
through group membership. We often hear principals refer to
staff members as though they were no more than a number of
discrete persons. This is, of course, true up to a point. It is also
true, however, that a staff consists of something which is greater
and more powerful than a mere collection of persons. A staff
is a group, or a number of groups. When St. Agatha's was
established many years ago, a staff of teachers was selected from
several parts of Australia. When they first arrived in the common room they stood uneasily around tables or covered up
their embarrassment by puffing at cigarettes. Gradually, however, they began to "jell", to find common interests, to share
confidences, to regard the school as more than a pile of bricks
and mortar. They became a group. As members of the group
the teachers developed into different kinds of individuals with
allegiances and loyalties and norms which they had not shared
earlier. This group, like a person, developed a power of its own,

a power with tremendous resources for good in the operation of the organization. It also developed an important communication network.

I suspect that, in independent schools, horizontal communication among teachers tends to be more effective than in state schools because of the common room system. In many state schools, by contrast, staff rooms are provided on a subject basis, or as separate rooms for men and women. Very rarely is a general common room seen in which all members of staff—young, old, male, female, senior, junior—come together as a staff for informal chatting and tea-drinking. The practice of deliberately breaking up a staff into small groups is so extraordinarily short-sighted as to make one wonder whether some state education departments are aware that there is such a thing as a horizontal communication, and that it can play a major role in the development of staff morale and professional involvement.

However, the common room is not only a prime conveyor of informal horizontal communication: it is also a very important channel of upward and downward communication. It is here that the head drinks his tea, mixes with teachers, gets the "feel" of the staff, hears gossip, and becomes a member of the group. Of course, if he prefers to drink his tea and munch his scones in splendid isolation, he misses out on what should be his most valuable channel of communication, his link, his finger on the *real* pulse of the school.

The hard fact of the situation is that the principal may accept the existence of the group and seek membership of it, or he may choose to ignore it. The act of joining it does *not* imply that the head has to be "one of the boys", on Christian name terms with all and sundry or that he gives up in any way his final responsibility for the operation of the school. It does mean, however, that he mixes with his staff, is well known to and by them, and that he shares, at least to some extent, their goals, their joys, and their fears.

So far I have argued for informal communication with the staff as a group.

Of equal importance is the *formal* organization of the staff as a work group. Now, a staff and principal are unlikely to work effectively as a group if they do not actually *meet* formally as a group. This can be effected only through the staff meeting.

A great deal has been written and said about staff meetings over the last few years.[14] I believe that this is a very healthy and very encouraging development, for as far as I can see the staff meeting provides a master key to the successful administration of today's schools.

There are, of course, staff meetings *and* staff meetings. There is a vast gap between the one-sided tirade and the work-group centred discussion. A group operates best when its goals are clearly defined and widely accepted, when its members can communicate with one another as equals, when its individual members feel that they have something to contribute to the realization of its goals. I am by no means alone in this point of view. *Education and the Democratic Ideal*[15] by an Englishman, A. G. Hughes, and *Supervision for Better Schools*[16] by K. Wiles, an American, are good examples of books which develop this theme.

The important thing is that a properly conducted, professional meeting, in which all feel free to express their minds, to vote, to be defeated, or to achieve success on issues close to their hearts, produces an involvement in the enterprise and releases a power which is probably not attainable by any other means.

Yet, in spite of all that we know about group dynamics, many Australian schools continue to be administered as though they were military organizations of a most rigid type, giving teachers little or no say in policy matters, in choice of curriculum, or even in choice of teaching methods. That this should be the case is quite extraordinary, for I can think of no group of professional people more likely to benefit from mutual discussion and decision making than teachers, who are normally adult, educated at a tertiary level, committed to teaching and prepared to go to considerable personal sacrifice in the interests of the children in their charge. Yet we so often treat these teachers as though they were half-wits, incapable of reaching even minor decisions either in groups or as individuals.

[25]

The implications of what I have said so far for decision making (how *does* the Head reach good decisions when only some of what is going on in his school is known to him?), communicating (how else can an organization be co-ordinated and evaluated?), morale building (is not organization maintenance as important as organization achievement?), and initiating change (how successfully is change initiated without staff support?) are obvious.

At the risk of pressing my point too hard, I wish to remind you that the principal is an executive who seeks to contribute to the maximum growth of every child and every teacher in his organization. He is not to drive, but lead; not to bully, but involve; not to demand, but to expect; not to enchain, but to free. I had better make myself very clear on one critical point: in advocating maximal formal and informal staff involvement in the enterprise I am not suggesting for a moment that the principal can delegate his final responsibility for the organization. Final responsibility *cannot* be shared.

ORGANIZATIONAL AUTHORITY AND RESPONSIBILITY

In practice authority and responsibility are inseparable. As Bierstedt has pointed out: "Where there is no organization, there is no authority and where there is no authority there is no organization".[17]

We recognize that in any organization, including schools, tasks are grouped or subdivided among the members of the organization and that levels of authority for the discharging of responsibilities are defined. This gradation is often referred to as the scalar principle or as the chain of command.

The delegation of authority and responsibility has interested many scholars, though most of what is known seems to be "commonsense" rather than "scientific" in nature. Several authors stress that in delegating his authority, the administrator in no wise divests himself of responsibility. Gregg[18] describes the delegation of authority as "an attempt by the administrator to arrange for the more effective use of the authority he holds". Knezevich points out that the responsibility for a task rests with the executive who delegated the duty as well as with the person who accepted it:

> It follows that the authority granted should be equal to the responsibility. It is unfair to hold a man accountable for results he is not permitted to guide according to his own best judgment.

Knezevich also stresses the importance of reporting:

> It is through accounting of or reporting on duties delegated and authorities granted that the executive is able to maintain the pulse of the institution in spite of his inability to specifically execute all the duties thrust upon him.[19]

This question of delegation is probably growing in importance. In New South Wales, for example, it is usual for the headmaster and the deputy to share responsibility for the supervision of teachers. This raises the question of how many teachers one man can be expected to formally supervise. Urwick would not hesitate to give an answer, "No superior can supervise directly the work of more than five or, at the most, six subordinates whose work interlocks".[20] Knezevich would reply, "There is no magic number . . . that represents the effective span of supervision for any and all executives . . ."[21] So far as I know, social science has not yet settled this difference of opinion!

ORGANIZATIONAL BEHAVIOUR

We cannot very well leave the question of organization without referring to the administrator's organizational behaviour.

At St. Agatha's the principal has by virtue of her position *ascribed* status, but she clearly lacks *earned* status or prestige; she is thus, in spite of her proud organization chart, only half an administrator. In any organization there are at least two key role dimensions—the personal and the institutional. And there are thus at least two aspects of leadership—that in which authority is granted and that in which authority is earned. *The effective principal is he who makes the granted authority effective through earned prestige.*

Guba[22] and Getzels[23] have developed a model or theory for use in the prediction and investigation of organizational be-

[27]

haviour. They argue that a school is a social system and that a social system involves two classes of phenomena:

a) the institutions with certain roles and expectations that will fulfil the goals of the system (the nomothetic dimension); and

b) the individuals with certain personalities and need-dispositions whose observed interaction we call social behaviour (the idiographic dimension).

The most important analytic units of an institution are *roles* which may be defined in terms of *expectations*, i.e. in terms of the rights, privileges, and obligations to which any incumbent of the role must adhere. Personality is the dynamic organization within the individual of these need-dispositions that govern his unique reactions to the environment and to expectations of his environment.

These two dimensions account for much organizational behaviour. On the institutional dimension the administrator defines roles, applies rewards or punishments, and makes decisions. Here his power is granted by the employing authority. On the personality dimension his status is *achieved*: he develops his prestige and influence on the basis of merit.

The administrator without power in *both* of these dimensions is very restricted. The martinet who rules through the first dimension alone is indeed a pitiful sight, but no more so than the mistakenly democratic leader who abdicates his granted responsibility and who tries to work through the idiographic dimension alone.

This is but one theory, but it provides an excellent entrée to the listing of some organizational problems which appear to have developed and multiplied over the years without any attention to any basic principle other than that of expediency.

SOME PROBLEMS FOR DISCUSSION

I shall now present some factual statements about schools. As I read them I shall ask myself: Does this organizational practice clearly

a) contribute to the liberation of the potentialities of the individual pupil and the individual teacher;

b) have some rationale other than tradition for its existence,

c) encourage good decision making,
d) encourage high staff morale,
e) encourage effective communication,
f) encourage successful initiation of change?
 Perhaps you, too, would like to ask yourselves these questions as the practices are listed one by one.

1. The school year begins without a preliminary staff meeting.
2. The school year begins without the principal's having any knowledge of the names, experience, and interests of the teachers newly appointed to his staff.
3. Separate staff rooms are provided for male and female teachers.
4. The home science and manual work staffs are the only teachers provided with separate staff rooms.
5. The headmaster always has morning tea and lunch in his office.
6. Staff meetings are held once each term.
7. Subject masters write detailed programmes for each member of their respective staffs.
8. The sports master is given instructions to organize a sports carnival but is warned against "railroading" teachers to assist him.
9. High school boys are taught separately from girls.
10. The headmaster announces "out of the blue" that he wants his staff to adopt a new composition marking scheme in a week's time.
11. It is decided to close seven one- and two-teacher schools to form a combined area school.
12. Newly arrived teachers are assigned retarded and troublesome classes.
13. The school possesses a policy book.
14. Classes are always kept as small as possible.
15. A very successful teacher is recommended for the post of principal.

CONCLUSION

 I raised these questions in conclusion because they all have implications for organizational change in certain schools—

perhaps your own. Obviously, an organization needs stability in order to survive, but survival in itself is no great gain if the organization has ceased, through rigidity, to achieve the purpose which society requires of it. Personally, I can see no argument for preserving an institution just because it calls itself a school. Of course, if that school has the clearly defined purpose of seeking to maximize the potentialities of its children and teachers and is constantly searching for means, teaching and administrative, to achieve this purpose, I see every argument for its preservation.

My point is, as Dimock puts it,[24] that good administration works in a groove, but not in a rut. Indeed, according to Jenson and Clarke this rut should never develop, because the administrative organization by its very structure should provide for the continuous and co-operative evaluation and redirection of the organization.[25]

Today, when society is changing so rapidly, it is essential that organizations—not the least educational organizations—have the flexibility to accommodate to these changes, as Lonsdale stresses, to initiate new structures or procedures, or to revise the goals of the organization. Stogdill[26] writes of a "median range within which flexibility and stability optimize the capacity for 'survival'". Clearly, this task calls not for mere administrators, but for administrators who are leaders as well.

THREE

TRAINING THE EDUCATIONAL ADMINISTRATOR

Adapted from a paper read at the Australian College of Education Seminar on Educational Administration, University of Western Australia, Perth, January 1965.

INTRODUCTION

When my old friend Mark Twain described a cauliflower as a cabbage with a college education he was implying that attendance at a college had in some way a profound effect on that humble vegetable. Without pushing the analogy too far (though in one or two cases I know of, it applies only too well), the protagonists of training for educational administrators claim that preparation at college is likely to have a profound effect on the administrative behaviour of those in executive positions in education.

In recent years there has appeared, particularly in the United States, a plethora of books and articles on this subject.[1] Australia too has produced its share of publications, including the deservedly widely-known *Training the Administrator*,[2] written for the Australian Council for Educational Research by Dr. Cunningham and Dr. Radford. This is an important report which merits the attention of all educators. Because it is so well known, I have deliberately avoided in this necessarily short paper several of the issues they raise and much of the information they present.

THE ARGUMENT FOR TRAINING

In the course of an earlier paper, I drew attention to the challenge of professionalism and asserted that the prime duty of the educational administrator was to facilitate the liberation of the potentialities of individual children and of individual teachers.

This duty or task, so directly stated, is deceptively simple. In fact, it represents a major exercise in human engineering—one which today taxes the minds and physical energies of some of the world's leading scholars in the field of education.

I should point out at this stage that much of what I have to say is pure rationalization. To the best of my knowledge there is not available any objective evidence to show whether trained administrators are any more effective than untrained administrators, or whether certain approaches to training are more effective than others. Of course, this is nothing very unusual in the sphere of education. For example, I know of no objective evidence to show that trained teachers are any more effective than untrained teachers, yet I am sure that there are few, if any, educators today who would oppose the pre-service and in-service training of teachers.

The argument for the training of administrators is little different from that advanced for the training of teachers, i.e., it is possible to learn most trades or professions (including, for example, medicine, engineering, or teaching) by apprenticeship, but we set out through the provision of preparatory courses to short circuit, to organize, to discipline if you prefer, knowledge which is likely otherwise to be mastered only after a prolonged, wasteful, and trial-and-error apprenticeship. Further, we hope that through attendance at advanced educational institutions the professional of tomorrow will come into contact with ideas which push his thinking to the frontiers of his calling and which may even inspire him to conduct research at a later stage of his career. In other words we try to avoid the in-breeding of ideas which apprenticeship may produce.

One of the most important arguments used to attack the pupil-teacher system in New South Wales at the beginning of the twentieth century was that the teacher learnt at the expense of his pupils. Most of us would, I think, agree that as far as possible doctors should not be allowed to learn at the expense of their patients or railway engineers at the expense of train travellers. It is but a short step from this argument to ask why, when we frown on teachers learning at the expense of their pupils, we apparently accept without question the practice of administrators learning at the expense of both pupils *and* teachers.

Of course, this argument is not one of black or white. We all know that doctors, engineers, and teachers do in fact learn at the expense of their clients and that this is an inevitable part of the learning process. However, we try to minimize this through well disciplined courses of training followed by more or less well supervised periods of probation or internship. Few of us really believe that a teachers' college produces a teacher, or a medical school a doctor, but most of us are prepared to admit that this pre-service education has given the candidate a very good start on his way to professional competence. This is the argument presented for the training of administrators—not that they should emerge from a course claiming to be professional administrators, but that they have a core of information, theories, experience, ethics, and ideals with which to begin practice.

So far we have argued for the training of educational administrators on the grounds of

a) short circuiting a lengthy apprenticeship,

b) need for forward-looking administrators and researchers, and

c) avoidance of trial and error learning at the expense of staff or clients.

All of these seem to me to boil down to making the maximum use, in a greatly reduced time, of scarce managerial resources. We need to ask ourselves whether our present practice of encouraging the trial-and-error "less-than-apprenticeship" style of training for administrative positions is in the interests of children, and indeed, of the nation. I suspect—and again, I have no objective evidence to support this contention—that, of all the institutions in our society, schools are most wasteful in their refusal to make use of the highly intelligent, dedicated, and skilled staff at their disposal.

[33]

TRAINING ADMINISTRATORS IN OTHER FIELDS

At this stage it may prove interesting to remind ourselves of the steps taken by industry, commerce, and the public services to introduce courses in administration or to support those already in existence. It would be a gross overstatement to claim that all leaders in industry, for example, were convinced of the value of courses for administrators, but we would be blind or worse if we closed our eyes to the very strong support given by industry to the Australian institutes of management, the technical colleges and institutes of technology, the Australian Administrative Staff College, and, more recently the postgraduate courses in business administration offered by Australian universities. Even British industry, one of the great strongholds of amateurism, has recently donated vast sums of money for the establishment of courses in business administration in two English universities.

From time to time in Britain, though by no means as commonly in Australia nowadays, eyebrows are raised when one refers to administration as a field for academic study. Perhaps the best answer to this is to draw the attention of the eyebrow raiser to the high academic rating of the Harvard Graduate School of Business Administration and the Harvard Graduate School of Education, both of which have taken the lead in developing training programmes in their respective spheres of interest for many years. Or one could just close one's eyes and patiently recite the words of Colonel Urwick, senior partner of the famous management consultant firm of Urwick, Orr, and Partners and author of a classic work in administration:[3]

> It is fifty years since commerce became academically respectable. But what is taught as commerce in most universities is merely the economics of yesterday and the bad habits of the managers of the day before yesterday . . . New "disciplines" are not invented. They develop from existing bodies of knowledge because in some respect these existing bodies of knowledge fail to provide answers to practical problems which are troubling men's minds.[4]

Our discussion up to this point has overlooked a rather serious complication which arises when the training of administrators is mooted. The complication arises from the fact that in most fields of endeavour the responsibilities of administration are thrust upon the individual only after he has demonstrated his skill in some other field. Thus, the successful accountant is appointed to the position of branch manager, the resident doctor to that of medical superintendent, the teacher to that of principal. Putting this in another way, few people enter a profession or trade with a view to becoming administrators. Thus they cannot, in Australian society today, enrol in, say, a technical college course in management as tyros and hope for managerial appointments. But there are exceptions to this as any observer of Royal Military College, Duntroon, or of the Royal Australian Naval College can testify.

A BRIEF HISTORY OF ADMINISTRATOR TRAINING

The training of educational administrators by other than trial and error and apprenticeship is a new concept in Australia. In the United States, as we have seen, it developed some decades ago. The story of the American development is well told by Dr. Jack Culbertson in the 1964 yearbook of the National Society for the Study of Education.[5] Culbertson, who is executive director of the influential University Council for Educational Administration, describes the early emphasis on job performance, which owed its inspiration to Frederick Taylor's classic *Principles of Scientific Management*,[6] first published in 1911. For Taylor the controlling aim was efficiency; men were cogs in the wheels of production; administration was concerned only secondarily with human considerations. Ellwood P. Cubberley,[7] the father of the study of educational administration, was obviously influenced by Taylor, comparing the school with a factory and viewing children as raw materials.

The conclusions reached by Elton Mayo[8] and his co-workers in the course of the famous Hawthorne experiments had an important influence on programmes for the preparation of administrators in most fields. These studies, which had commenced as attempts to improve efficiency in the Taylor sense, demonstrated convincingly the importance of human relationships in administration. As Culbertson puts it, organizations were seen, not so much as rational instruments which could be neatly depicted in charts, but as dynamos of human energies and motivations, many of which were irrational in character.[9]

Just after World War II the "human relations" approach became intimately associated with the rather abstruse notion of "democratic administration" or "involvement administration". In fine, this association tended to produce an acceptance of the importance of staff involvement in the interests of human satisfactions, morale, efficiency, and the furtherance of democratic principles. This, generally, was the prevailing theory in the one or two Australian university courses in educational administration introduced in 1959. In fact, this approach provided the central theme for the first edition of Bassett, Crane, and Walker's *Headmasters for Better Schools*.[10]

The scientific movement in administration probably dates from Simon's *Administrative Behavior*, first published in 1947,[11] though some would say that the seminal book was Barnard's classic *Functions of the Executive*, dating from 1938.[12] A few of those concerned with the training of educational administrators first became aware of this movement with the establishment of the National Conference of Professors of Educational Administration in 1947 and of the Co-operative Program in Educational Administration, heavily endowed by the W. K. Kellogg Foundation in 1950. Most teachers in the field, however, including the few Australians interested, knew little of this movement until the publication of a number of influential books in the late 1950's, including Halpin's *Administrative Theory in Education*,[13] Griffith's *Administrative Theory*,[14] and Campbell and Gregg's *Administrative Behavior in Education*.[15]

This movement, which owed much to Waldo's logical positivism, in its extreme form "abhors metaphysics, dismisses ethics, emphasizes empiricism, places a high premium upon rigorous, logical analysis".[16] Some professors refused to discuss "shoulds" or values, asking only what "is". Australian scholars of educational administration, though recognizing the "is" of administration, as I pointed out in an earlier paper, and placing a high value on theory, have rarely lost sight completely of the "oughts". Nor have they ignored the obvious importance of some aspects of Taylor's "efficiency" and Mayo's "human relations". Courses are developed on a broader base than previously, and while the aim is the preparation of a leader who is a skilled decision maker gifted in communication skills and analytical powers and well versed in the applications of theories, it has not usually been forgotten that administration must remain in part an idealistic venture performed in a setting where there are many conflicting issues and views. This balanced view, I believe, represents the approach to the study and teaching of educational administration in the best American and Australian institutions today.

SOME ISSUES

Having reviewed briefly the history of the ideas underlying the training movement, I wish now to raise certain issues which are relevant to my case, and to discuss each of them briefly. Let us look at them *seriatim*. You may consider some of them repetitious, but I am anxious to clear up each point as we proceed, in the hope of presenting a logical argument.

Is there a case for training educational administrators?

I think that all I have said so far asserts loud and clear that there is such a case. I have argued this on the grounds of the most effective and economical use, in the interests of children and of the nation, of our resources of personnel and material.

Surely there is at least as convincing a case for the training of executives in education as there is in business or the armed services, or do we believe, as I sometimes suspect, that business and the army are more important to us than schools, and hence are worthy of more skilled administrators?

What should the student be taught in such courses?

Culbertson[17] claims that decision making, communicating, morale building, and initiating change are important aspects of administration, and hence should be included in the curriculum, together with a number of other areas, including scientific concepts, values as seen in the humanities, and trends in econo-

[37]

mics, politics, and sociology. Culbertson is, of course, referring to the content of the postgraduate courses taken by budding or practising administrators at the master's and doctor's level in American universities.

Perhaps you may be interested to know something of the thinking which underlay the curriculum for the University of New England's postgraduate Diploma in Educational Administration when it was introduced in 1959. The details of this development were presented to a seminar in Canberra recently (see Chapter 5).

As can readily be seen from that paper, we aim to provide some basic information on individual children and adults in organizational settings, and to look at this behaviour in a sociological, historical, and comparative setting. The written exercises, seminars, residential schools, and dissertation all seek to challenge the administrator to look incisively at himself, his school, and his school system.

Does the course succeed in satisfying the criteria implied in the principles I read out to you earlier? Only time will tell. Certainly we have some very enthusiastic diplomates. Their comments, I am flattered to report, are not very different from the first report on Mark Twain's death, i.e. "somewhat exaggerated".

It is important to note that I am referring to a postgraduate diploma restricted to applicants with at least a first degree and several years experience in teaching and administration. If we were designing an undergraduate qualification or a postgraduate degree to follow the diploma, the pattern would be a little different, though I think that in general we would preserve the above objectives, just as we have done as far as possible in our courses for the degree of Bachelor of Letters, for example.

At what stage should the student take his courses?

Views differ on this. Applicants for enrolment in the University of New England's diploma courses must have had considerable experience in teaching or administration. In practice this has meant more than ten years' teaching for many candidates (considerably more in the majority of cases), though there have been occasional candidates with only six or seven years' teaching experience. At that University the study of educational administration is limited to the postgraduate level only, with a course diploma, a course and research degree of Bachelor of Letters, or a research degree only: Master of Arts or Doctor of Philosophy.

Sydney University, too, restricts the study of educational administration to graduates, but the other Australian universities permit some work in their undergraduate Bachelor of Education programmes. So far as I can ascertain, such undergraduate students are, however, usually teachers or principals attempting a first degree comparatively late in life. Armidale Teachers' College has plans to introduce an external course in educational administration for non-graduates, and I gather that some sort of experience qualification will be required.

I should say, at this stage, my belief is that, in Australia at present and in the foreseeable future, courses in administration should properly be restricted to students who have a professional qualification (not necessarily a university degree) in a field like medicine, engineering, or teaching, or who can demonstrate some experience in their chosen fields.

I must confess that I have little regard for a proposal now being openly championed by several academics who each year attend the inter-disciplinary seminar on Administrative Studies arranged by the Research School of Social Sciences at the Australian National University. This is a proposal for a first degree to be known as a Bachelor of Administration. I do not consider it impossible to design a degree which would provide a core of administrative studies *per se*, and which included a solid selection of specialist options in say, public, business, or educational administration, but I would prefer not to do so at the present stage of our development.

At the moment I cannot quite see how the recipient of such a degree would fit into Australian schools, though I could see a very bright future for a young man who spent six or seven years in taking the joint degrees of Bachelor of Education and Bachelor of Administration, a practice not unknown in other professional circles. Certainly I can see a place for a Master of Administration degree which provides for a core of general administrative studies and for specialization in such areas as educational or hospital administration.

How should the student be taught?

Administration, like teaching or medicine, involves active participation in planning, co-ordinating, communicating, diagnosing, decision making, and so on. Students of administration, like those of teaching or medicine, are anxious to sink their teeth into courses and experiences which are real to them and which clearly have relevance to the practice of their profession. They tend to be impatient with theory as it is usually presented to them—an understandable and inevitable consequence of teaching which does not demonstrate clearly the unity of theory and practice.

I am sure that the traditional methods of university teaching —lectures, tutorials, and seminars—will continue to play an important role in the preparation of professionals in every sphere. These techniques provide unequalled opportunities for the presentation of information, the joint solution of problems, and the cross-fertilization of ideas. I am equally convinced, however, that these methods are sterile if they are not closely linked to the real-life world of administration as the student sees it.

In a diploma course like that at New England, the question of a practical link with the real-life world is taken care of to a large extent by the fact that all of the students have had at least some experience in the administration of schools or departments of schools. They quickly see the relevance of their course work to their professional task, and any lecturer who is not capable of demonstrating this relevance is rapidly pulled into line by his students. I am not suggesting that such students should not be brought into regular and constant contact with everyday administration, whether simulated or real—merely that for such students this is much less of a problem than for those who would enrol in, for example, the proposed Bachelor of Administration course without experience in administration.

Generally speaking, methods of instruction which seek to relate emerging concepts to practice (in the hope, let us admit, of improving the latter and testing the former) may be divided into two: simulated situations and actual situations. In my view there is a place for both of these approaches in all courses of preparation, although the content and emphasis will obviously vary according to the experience and qualifications of the particular student population.

For a moment, let us look briefly at each of these approaches.

Simulated situations

A few years ago Daniel Griffiths of New York University wrote an excellent assessment of the case method of teaching for the *Journal of Educational Administration*.[18] The case method presents the student with a chunk of reality, often drawn from the experience of its author, with all the pertinent information required for reaching a decision. Originally, cases were used to provide a variety of administrative experiences and to afford opportunities for decision making, but in recent years their worth in demonstrating theory has been widely recognized.

Cases were first used for preparing administrators in the Harvard Graduate School of Business Administration in the 1920's, but their use in the training of educational administrators did not become widespread until the late 1950's. Two important pioneering collections of case studies were those of Sargent and Belisle (1955),[19] and Culbertson, Jacobson, and Reller (1960).[20] In recent years the University Council for Educational Administration[21] has put a great deal of effort and expense into the development of cases, and has had them taped and filmed, as well as printed in the usual way. The first Australian collection of case studies has been published by the University of Queensland Press.[22]

Simulated materials proper are really a development from the case. Perhaps the best known simulated situations were those developed for the Whitman School in the important "in-basket" project reported as *Administrative Performance and Personality*.[23] The student is given a clear account of the simulated school through films, recordings, and printed material. He is then presented with an "in-basket" containing items with which he must make decisions: letters, memoranda, telephone calls, notes, news clippings, and so on. Obviously, this technique provides countless opportunities for students assuming the role of principal to make decisions on a wide range of human, technical, and conceptual problems. So far as is known, this method has not yet been adopted in more than an elementary way in Australian institutions preparing educational administrators.

As its use becomes more widespread, I hope we shall keep in mind the rather pathetic plea of one American:

> A student of administration with tact
> Learned all the answers he lacked
> But acquiring a job,
> He said with a sob,
> How do you fit answers to fact?[24]

Real-life situations

These situations include the field study and the internship. The field study has been used to some extent at Armidale, particularly in the course of residential school visits to high schools and other institutions, and in dissertation projects. Such studies provide opportunities for students to observe, analyse, and evaluate administration as an on-going task.

As far as I can ascertain, the internship has not yet been employed in Australia. This method provides for the potential administrator to be given actual administrative responsibility while under the direct supervision of skilled practitioners and university teachers. Obviously, this approach has its equivalent in the medical internship and to a much less satisfactory extent in the probationary period experienced by teachers who have just completed their professional training. The internship appears to offer unparalleled opportunities for helping the administrator make the transition from preparation to practice, in assisting him to develop technical skills, and in obtaining experience in diagnosing problems related to, for example, decision making, morale, and communication. This economical method (in the sense that it avoids much of the trial and error learning we spoke of earlier) has much to commend it, and I suspect that we shall hear a good deal about it in the next few decades.

In an earlier paper, I drew attention to the dangers of the development of a managerial elite who, though trained in administration *per se*, might have little appreciation of the school's mission to society. This is a challenge which must be faced sooner or later. The answer to this challenge I leave to you.

Whatever answer is found, it will be essential that the administrator be aware of the two key facts of social change and individual differences, that he realize with Sir Percy Nunn that "The idea that the main aim of the school is to socialize its pupils in no wise contradicts the view that its true aim is to cultivate individuality".[25]

As I pointed out in a recent publication:

> The aims of education as distinct from instruction are achieved *through the efforts of individual teachers interacting with individual children*. Each child reacts to ideas in his own way. The master teacher sets out to interact with each child in such a manner as to arouse his interest and enthusiasm while contributing to his knowledge and understanding. This educative relationship, aimed at releasing the full potential of the individual pupil, is based not on mere physical proximity, but on personal interaction. It is at its best when the teacher feels free to adapt his teaching to the individual's peculiar interests and needs.
>
> In practice, all of this means that there must be an accepted body of knowledge and values, but at the same time the freedom to challenge this knowledge and values; routines, but opportunities for breaking routines; syllabuses but freedom to depart from syllabuses; accepted methods, but freedom to experiment with methods; traditions, but freedom to question traditions.
>
> Since it is a function of administration to provide the organisation within which individual teachers and individual children interact, the achievement of this nice balance be-

tween the accepted and the questioned, the routine and the flexible, the prescribed and the suggested is the proper duty of the administrator.[26]

I cannot see any one solution or any one theory which will serve to produce excellence in the administration of our schools. As Halpin has pointed out:

> When confronted with different "knowings" the naive person is tempted to ask, "which is more real? Which is *really* the truth?" This question is just as rhetorical, just as futile today as it once was in the mouth of Pontius Pilate.[27]

A few months ago Professor W. F. Connell of Sydney University, speaking on the Australian Broadcasting Commission's programme "News Review", referred to the lack of adventurousness in Australian schools. He was referring to teaching and curriculum, but his criticism might just as easily have been aimed at administration. We *are* a stodgy profession, but I see no one good reason why we should remain that way. Most of us would rather, I suspect, be one of Mark Twain's adventurous cauliflowers than one of his stodgy cabbages.

FOUR

THE ADMINISTRATIVE REVOLUTION :
THE ROLE OF THE UNIVERSITY

Adapted from an article in the *Australian Journal of Higher Education* I, no. 2, (1963), pp. 89-97. Reprinted by permission of the editor.

The school is a unique institution in our society.[1] Not only is it the only institution charged with the transmission of the *mores*[2]—those aspects of our culture which we regard as most worthy of preservation—but it is the only institution which aims at presenting to the young an objective assessment of issues which are crucial to our culture. It seeks to present to the child, irrespective of his creed, colour, or status, that which is best in our culture in such a manner as to lead him to think critically and perceptively. The fact that so many schools do not apparently achieve these ends is not relevant to the argument. Certainly these are the purposes for which schools exist if our curricula and such significant publications as the Norwood,[3] Harvard,[4] and Wyndham[5] reports are to be taken seriously.

Further, the school is unique in that children *must* attend. In a very real sense the state has usurped the traditional power of the father over his child so far as schooling is concerned. The father can still choose whether or not to send his boy to church, whether or not to enrol him in the Boy Scouts, but he cannot choose whether or not to send him to school. The school thus has a particular relationship with, and responsibility to, the state, the community, and the parent. There is probably no other public institution which is quite so all-pervading, which touches so many lives, which is so much in the public eye.

The fundamental importance of this institution to our society should lead us to ask searching questions about the quality of the men who have been selected to administer our schools and school systems. What might we expect of such a man? At the very least we would expect him to be aware of the unique function of the school in society, to recognize that his school exists not merely for the good of the community and the state but also for the good of the child, to have a scholarly interest in one or more fields of academic interest, to have demonstrated his skill as a teacher, and to have thought profoundly about the administration of a school as an educative institution.

The reference to administration was deliberately placed last in the list of expectations, not because it is relatively un-important—in fact it is of crucial importance—but because it is not possible to conceive of the administration of an *educative community*[6] as distinct from an *instructional institution* unless the other expectations are met.

So long as schools were small and teachers and pupils alike were known intimately to headmasters, it was probably not so important that the headmaster should concern himself with administrative theory. However, with increasing size, special-ization, and departmentalism, the possibility of the school developing as an educative community is becoming more and more remote.[7] Communication among departments is often difficult, subject specialists tend to pay attention to only those aspects of school life which impinge directly on their own interests, children become increasingly distant from the head-master and his senior officers—the school becomes little more than an instructional factory.

Clearly, Australian schools are no longer the simple organ-izations of the nineteenth century in which a small group of poorly qualified, underpaid teachers, assisted by "pupil teachers", clicked their heels to the omnipotent head and taught to a restrictive syllabus which specified the standards to be achieved. It is not unusual now to find in an Australian country town a high school, which cost nearly a million dollars, ad-ministered by a headmaster who is responsible for a thousand children, forty teachers divided into many departments, two secretarial assistants, a home science maid, a school farm labourer, a janitor, and several part-time cleaners and a canteen manager. Unlike the executives of most other institutions, the headmasters of schools are little concerned with junior or non-professional employees. The great mass of workers with whom the school principal is concerned have experienced a tertiary education, sometimes more advanced than his own, enjoy life tenure, have rather fixed ideas on what should and should not be taught, and belong to highly-organized industrial associations. There are few institutions which present so many opportunities for "working with" rather than "working for" than the school, and yet there is probably no institution in which the potentialities of this unique situation remain so blatantly unrecognized.

In recent years, interest in educational administration has grown greatly, both in the United States and Australia and to a lesser extent in Britain. As schools have become larger, principals have been freed from class teaching. At the same time the work of university departments of Public Administration and Business Administration has become more widely known. The relative novelty of the field is shown by the fact that in that land of great "joiners"—the United States—the National Conference of Professors of Educational Administration was not established until 1947.

The study of educational administration in the United States, however, dates from the first decade of the twentieth century. As indicated in Chapter 3, it developed to a large extent from the "scientific management" movement led by Frederick W. Taylor in America and Henri Fayol in France. Although Taylor's *Principles of Scientific Management*[8] and Fayol's *Administration Industrielle et Generale*[9] took a narrow view of management, stressing organizational processes and tending to ignore the psychological aspects of mobilizing human effort, they attracted a great deal of attention. The earlier educational administration textbooks of Cubberley and Strayer, for example, adopted what was essentially a "job analysis" approach.

The human relations aspect of administration, developed by Mary Parker Follett[10] in the 1920's and convincingly supported by the evidence produced by Elton Mayo[11] in the course of his Hawthorne experiments in the 1930's, persuaded theorists

[47]

in administration that "what goes on inside the worker is even more significant for production than what goes on outside". In the late 1930's Chester Barnard's *Functions of the Executive*[12] sought to tie together the "organization achievement" and the "individual satisfaction" theories through an analysis of formal and informal organization.

The postwar years produced a great deal of theoretical and empirical work in the field of educational administration, much of it sponsored by the seven million dollar Co-operative Program in Educational Administration underwritten by the W. K. Kellogg Foundation in both the United States[13] and Canada.[14] The influence of Taylor, Follett, Mayo, and Barnard was reflected in the educational textbooks of the period, but increasing emphasis was placed on the implications for the administrative process of social psychology and sociology. Research into the psychology of leadership and "leadership behaviour" produced some suggestive results, notably in the work of Halpin and Hemphill at Ohio State University.[15] From all this activity there emerged no over-riding theory of administration. However, the period has produced the first serious efforts to investigate educational administration as a unique aspect of administration; it has made school leaders painfully aware of the need for constant evaluation of their ideas and it has added fuel to the long-standing argument whether administration is an art or a science.[16]

In the United States, one outcome of all this activity has been the development of university courses in educational administration. Such courses are almost invariably offered at the graduate level, both for young men wishing to become school administrators and for those practising administrators who wish to improve their qualifications. So highly regarded are these courses that a great many school districts will not employ a superintendent or principal unless he has made some progress towards a higher degree in the field.

It is important to note that the best of these courses are not designed to *train* administrators in a "how-to-do-it" pattern, to provide answers to individual problem situations, but to provide insights into organizational behaviour generally. The latter approach is by far the more promising and by far the more logical. Clearly, administration is an interaction situation involving people. To assert that there is only one way of administering an institution would be as ludicrous as to assert that there is only one way of teaching children arithmetic. It is patent that, while there are administrative theories and techniques to be learned, the application of these will depend very much upon the personality and philosophy of the administrator and upon the situation in which he finds himself.

With regard to Australia an interesting analogy may be drawn between the preparation of teachers a half century ago and the preparation of administrators today. Until 1910 in New South Wales and until much later in other Australian states, it was assumed that the best means of producing teachers was to train young people "on the job". The pupil-teacher system, or some variation of it, survived for one hundred years in Australia. Today most of us reject this concept of "apprenticeship" of teachers as being narrow—conducive to inbreeding of ideas and contrary to modern professional practice. We describe the system as one which trains the teacher "at the expense of the pupil". So strong has been the reaction against this concept that there is a growing body of opinion which calls for the complete separation of the student teacher from the authority which will later employ him. In Britain and the United States most teachers are now educated in universities or in institutions which are closely affiliated with universities.

Most Australian school systems, however, remain suspicious of "academic" preparation for administrative roles. We have been content to assume that experience and its usual concomitant, seniority, breed administrative prowess. In fact, these factors might do no more than breed a gerontocracy remarkable for its routinized management;[17] certainly they are unlikely to breed administrators of insight and flexibility. This is not to imply that experience by itself or age by itself is any necessary hazard to effective administration, but it does imply that these may prove to be hazards if, as seems too common in our school systems, they are associated with administrative and intellectual stagnation.

[49]

Of all institutions, schools can least afford to stagnate. It is axiomatic that education thrives on controversy but there is little evidence of controversy in the government of Australian schools. The urge to work to the rules and regulations rather than to look for areas of freedom and responsibility casts a pall over the very institutions which should be experimenting, questioning, and theorizing. This attitude, so often remarked upon by observers from overseas,[18] can hardly be blamed solely upon centralization, although it is apparently more difficult to achieve variety, adaptability, and flexibility in a huge centralized system than in a number of small decentralized systems.[19] Recently a group of sixty Australian teachers was asked to indicate their experience outside of the particular school system in which they worked. Not one of the group had taught in, or so much as visited, schools in other Australian states; none had observed schools overseas; and only two had taught in another school system within their home state.

Despite our lack of "lighthouse" schools, however, there are signs that interest in educational administration in Australia is growing. Leadership appears to be coming from university departments of education and from some senior state departmental officers who have returned from journeys abroad. This interest is reflected in the growing demand for literature in the field, in the increasing support by headmasters of post-college and in-service courses and in the provision by universities of courses in educational administration.

In some states booksellers report a consistent demand for the many American and few British publications in the field. Interest in Australian publications is also growing. The proceedings of the University of Queensland's 1961 Conference on Educational Administration had a ready sale among headmasters.[20] During 1962 a symposium on "The School Principal", edited by O. R. Jones,[21] appeared and early in 1963 the University of Queensland Press published Bassett, Crane, and Walker's *Headmasters for Better Schools*.[22] The interest of other Australian publishers is obvious. A trickle of journal articles in the field has appeared in recent years, while such periodicals as the New South Wales State Education Department's *Leader* have provided headmasters with new sources of opinion and information.

There is, too, a tendency for state departments of education to send their senior officers to courses for administrators like those offered at the Australian Administrative Staff College in Victoria and by the New South Wales Public Service Board at the University of New South Wales. Such courses, though of inestimable value to the participants, are not normally available to administrators below top executive level. For the great majority of school principals, inspectors and the like, the post-college or in-service courses provided by teachers' colleges and state departments must suffice. Unfortunately, these courses are usually quite short in duration and often (though not always) are taught by practising departmental administrators who do little more than stress the virtues of existing practices.

Clearly, for the development of disciplined study of adminis-tration, for the definition of administrative theory, and for the influx of new ideas, we must look beyond the state education departments to the universities. If we accept the contention that the school is the key to the transmission of the cultural heritage, that it is nourished by controversy, and that the headmaster's prime concern is the development of an educative community, it seems clear that those who are administering our schools should be brought into close contact with the one institu-tion in our society which emphasizes cultural heritage, con-troversy, and education as distinct from instruction—the university.

Most of us would agree that it is not the function of a uni-versity to give training in mere management techniques or to concern itself with supervisor training. Courses of this type are best taught in technical colleges or in some of the in-service courses referred to above. Already, as Ortega y Gasset has so convincingly argued,[23] our universities have strayed too far from their historic mission towards the production of thorough-ly trained but ill-educated practitioners of the learned profes-sions. Where the university is concerned, techniques of school management are important only in so far as they relate to theories of administration which seek the achievement of an educative community.

British Commonwealth universities have accepted administration as a proper field of study not only for graduates but for undergraduates as well. Already Australian universities are offering or planning courses in Public Administration, Hospital Administration, and Business Administration. Some of these appear to be too much concerned with management techniques to win the approval of Australian members of Faculties of Arts, including the present author. Nevertheless, there is a demand for such courses. L. F. Urwick, for example, one of the best-known authors in the field of management, has presented a convincing case for the teaching of management in universities in his recent booklet, *Management*.[24] It is worthwhile repeating, however, that the argument in the present paper is that management study is important only in so far as it assists men of broad vision—men who control institutions which strive to transmit what is best in our culture—to effectively pass on some of their vision to their colleagues and to the children for whom the school exists.

Given the opportunity of developing a university course for educational administrators, what kind of course would you devise? This was the problem which faced a small group of members of the Armidale Teachers' College and the University of New England, including the present author, early in 1959. For what they are worth, the ideas which guided the introduction of the University of New England's course leading to the Diploma in Educational Administration are presented in Chapter 5.

Our experience suggests that the university more than any other institution can lead the administrator to think deeply and to read widely about the concept of an educative community. This is the aim of the graduate work leading to the Diploma in Educational Administration, the degrees of Bachelor of Letters, Bachelor of Education, Master of Arts, and Doctor of Philosophy offered at the University of New England, the graduate seminar available to the Master of Education students at the University of Sydney, and the proposed graduate and undergraduate Bachelor of Education courses of the University of Queensland.

Already such courses are leading some administrators, like their American colleagues of a decade ago, to recognize the poverty of theory in their field, the "naked empiricism" of research to date. In the United States, scholarly attempts have been made by such workers as Griffiths,[25] Parsons,[26] and Coladarci and Getzels[27] to examine the basis of administrative theory. More recently Lucio and McNeil[28] have attempted to analyse supervision—an important aspect of administration—as a synthesis of thought and action.

For too long, we in Australian schools and school systems have been concerned with recipes for action rather than with processes of thinking. We have taken for granted those stereotyped administrative procedures which have stressed line and staff organization, hierarchical administration, and routine efficiency but which have avoided experimentation, creative thought, controversy, and staff involvement in the school. Only now are we becoming aware of our own shortcomings.

It is part of the mission of the University to ensure that any changes or reforms which grow out of this new soul-searching are not permitted to become, in their turn, routinized and stereotyped. The men and women who are charged with the responsibility of administering our key social institution need constant reminders that understanding the administrative process is at least as difficult as understanding Einstein's watch. As Einstein puts it:

> In our endeavour to understand reality we are somewhat like a man trying to understand the mechanism of a closed watch. He sees the face and the moving hands, even hears it ticking, but he has no way of opening the case. If he is ingenious he may form some picture of a mechanism which would be responsible for all the things he observes, but he may never be quite sure his picture is the only one which would explain his observations.[29]

FIVE

DIPLOMA IN EDUCATIONAL ADMINISTRATION OF THE UNIVERSITY OF NEW ENGLAND

Adapted from a paper read at the second Seminar on Administrative Studies in the Research School of Social Sciences, Australian National University, Canberra, August 1964. This paper is reproduced essentially as it was read in 1964 *and is of interest as a historical case study only*. There have been substantial changes in the courses described and in the student body since this paper was prepared. Further, a Master's degree in educational administration has been introduced as a stepping stone to the Doctorate.

INTRODUCTION

This short background paper is intended to provide some essential facts about the postgraduate Diploma in Educational Administration programme of the University of New England. It does not describe facilities available for study in the area of educational administration for the University of New England's degrees of Bachelor of Letters, Bachelor of Education, Master of Arts, or Doctor of Philosophy, nor does it describe courses in educational administration offered by other Australian universities. Elsewhere I have placed the programme into the general setting of teaching and research in educational administration in Australia[1] and have argued for the teaching of educational administration by universities.[2] Further, I have described the part that such courses might play in affecting practice[3] and the emphasis that they might give to theory.[4] The programme has been described in a publication of the Australian Council for Educational Research,[5] and two books—one a text,[6] the other a collection of case studies[7]—have been written with the needs of the programme in mind.

[54]

The Diploma in Educational Administration is the only "named" qualification in educational administration offered by an Australian or New Zealand university. First offered in 1959, the diploma is now held by fifty-five Australian educators (approximately one half of those who enrolled in the programme during 1959–63). Though originally restricted to external students resident in New South Wales, the courses are now open to both full-time and external students resident in any state or territory of the Commonwealth. Unlike most university courses in administration, which are offered within Faculties of Commerce, this course is taught within the Faculty of Arts.

ORIGINS

The proposal to establish a postgraduate qualification in educational administration was made in 1958 to the University of New England and the New South Wales Education Department by Professor G. W. Bassett, at that time Principal of the Armidale Teachers' College and Acting Professor of Education at the University. After receiving approval from both bodies, Professor Bassett sought staff to teach the new course. I was contacted while in the United States and it was suggested that on my return to Australia I might assist in the planning and teaching of the new diploma.

With this aim in mind I spent the latter months of 1958 investigating, with the aid of a Carnegie Travel Grant, various aspects of educational administration, including teaching in the area, in a number of United States, Canadian and British centres. (No university courses in educational administration were observed in Britain, however.)

On arrival in Armidale, I submitted a plan for the diploma based very largely on Masters' programmes offered by leading North American universities. The plan was amended in discussion with Professor Bassett (now Professor and Dean of the Faculty of Education at the University of Queensland) and Mr. A. R. Crane (now Vice-Principal of Armidale Teachers' College) and the existing (1964) diploma programme remains substantially the product of the 1959 deliberations. Likewise, teaching towards the diploma remains a joint enterprise between the Department of Education at the University of New England and the Armidale Teachers' College.

It was agreed that the course should include three major sections:

a) foundation courses,

b) professional courses,

c) a field of special study for the candidate, probably in the form of a research project or minor dissertation.

During 1964 important changes in course content were approved by the Faculty of Arts. The new regulations will apply from the beginning of 1965.

GUIDING PRINCIPLES

From the beginning a number of basic principles were accepted to guide the planning and the development of the diploma. These were:

a) The diploma was essentially a qualification for practising administrators.

b) The diploma was not to be regarded as a "how to do it" qualification; rather was it to present the student with a variety of theories of administration which he might either put into practice or reject as he saw fit.

c) The diploma was to emphasize the universality of administrative tasks, to demonstrate the existence not only of an "adjectival" administration but of administration *qua* administration.

d) The diploma was to widen the vision and experiences of administrators whose experiences had been, in the main, restricted to particular types of schools or school systems.

e) The diploma was to emphasize that educational administration exists not in its own right, but as a service function to meet the needs of students and of society as a whole.

f) The diploma was to lead the student to appreciate that in the area of educational administration, research has barely scratched the surface of knowledge.

g) The diploma was to lead the student to see the importance of the development of a theory or theories of administrative behaviour upon which research and practice might be based.

h) The diploma was to provide the student with an opportunity to undertake minor research studies relating directly, where possible, to his own organizational environment.

THE DIPLOMA COURSES IN OPERATION

Prerequisites for enrolment

1. Candidates are required to hold at least a first university degree. Undergraduate or postgraduate work in Education or Public Administration is regarded as an advantage.

    In fact, many students have held more than one degree (there have been several Masters' degrees and a sprinkling of Doctorates) and many have held a Diploma in Education or a Bachelor of Education.

2. Candidates must have had considerable experience in teaching or administration.

    In practice this has been interpreted to mean

a) that the applicant holds an administrative post, e.g. inspector, superintendent, principal, deputy principal, subject master, registrar, deputy registrar, or

b) that he has been teaching sufficient years to make his appointment to such a position likely. In most Australian Education Departments this implies about ten years' teaching experience beyond completion of professional training.

A few candidates with less than ten years' experience have been enrolled but the mean number of years spent in teaching or administration is almost seventeen. Candidates have been drawn from state and independent schools, the universities, teachers', technical, and agricultural colleges, and from the armed services.

Time limits

Full-time students may attempt to complete the diploma in one year, the maximum time permitted being three years from initial enrolment.

Part-time and external students may not attempt to complete the diploma in less than two years. The maximum time they are permitted is four years from initial enrolment.

[57]

Course requirements 1964

At present candidates are required to complete eight courses, each of which is roughly equivalent to about one half of an undergraduate final year course, so the work load is equivalent to about four advanced undergraduate courses (plus the dissertation, which will be described later).

The courses are divided as follows:

Foundation courses

Each of these provides a foundation in certain areas of education, but differs from traditional foundation courses in looking at the areas studied from the point of view of the administrator rather than that of the teacher.

The courses are:

1. *The School in Society*, which looks at the social function of the school and examines some of the crucial issues in education, past and present, e.g. relationships between church and state, general versus special education.
2. *Development of Administrative Practices*, which is an historical-comparative study of the development of educational institutions and practices in Australia, England, and the United States, e.g. the growth of centralizing and decentralizing tendencies, state control of curricula, state inspection, and supervision.
3. *Mental Health and Education*, which examines aspects of the child's personality development, the socialization of his behaviour, teacher-pupil relationships, and common classroom problems of children.
4. *Measurement and Evaluation*, which introduces some common statistical techniques and discusses such problems as the evaluation of the teaching-learning process, the reliability of examinations, and the use of standardized tests.

Professional courses

These courses seek to introduce the student to a study of administration as an academic discipline. While the particular problems of educational administration are noted, the universality of administration is stressed, and throughout the course emphasis is placed on *theory* and *comparison*.

The courses are:

5. *Nature of Leadership*, which is largely concerned with a study of group dynamics, communication networks, staff morale, power structure, and leadership behaviour.

6. *Leadership in Practice*, which consists in the main of the study of classic writings in both administration in general and in educational administration. Follett, Barnard, Urwick, Tead, Simon, and Argyris are read as widely as their "educational" counterparts, Sears, Halpin, Campbell, Getzels, and Griffiths. Decision making and action taking are discussed and some use is made of the case study method.

7. *Comparative Administration*, which compares the effect upon administration of such controls as law, finance, curriculum, and politics in a number of countries. Evaluation of staff, provision of pupil personnel services, methods of keeping up to date, etc., are discussed from a comparative viewpoint.

8. *School Organization*, which looks at accounting procedures, office organization, use of plant, school architecture, and health services.

Candidates are required to purchase a substantial collection of books, the nucleus of a professional library, and to subscribe to four or five journals of which three are published overseas.

Dissertation

The dissertation is designed not only to arouse an interest in research in the field, but also to contribute something to our store of knowledge of theory and practice. The works have ranged over a wide area, some being empirical, others historical or comparative, a few theoretical. Some of the topics approved include "A Study of the Morale of a Sample of High School Teachers", "The Organization and Administration of Catholic Education in the Archdiocese of Canberra–Goulburn", "Organization and Methods in Office Management in High Schools", "A High School Staff as a Group", "The Achievement of the Stated Social Aims of an Independent School", and "Communication in a Large High School".

Course requirements 1965

As from 1965 candidates will read in four areas only. The courses will be known as Educational Administration, A B, C, and D respectively. Each course will consist of two strands, the former of which might be roughly termed "foundation", the latter "professional". This means that whereas in the past the foundation courses have been completed before enrolment in the professional courses, in the future candidates will read in areas which combine both emphases.

Educational Administration A, a course in comparative educational administration, examines the social and historical foundations of contemporary systems of education in certain Western societies. The first strand looks at the historical and social foundations of education in each of these societies up to the mid-nineteenth century. The second consists of comparative historical studies of the development of educational institutions and administrative practices in Australia, England, and the United States, particularly since the mid-nineteenth century.

Educational Administration B, which is concerned with the educational process and its assessment, examines the influence of various social institutions on the development of the individual and the implications of individual differences for educational administration. The first strand studies the development of the individual in a social system and looks at education as a process of cultural transmission, while the second strand consists of an introduction to the assessment of the pupil and the administrative implications of individual differences.

Educational Administration C is subtitled "Organizations: Theory and Applications" and is concerned with the implications of organization theory for educational administrators. The first strand introduces the theory of organizations while the second is concerned with the organization of educational systems and institutions. Strand two provides the candidate with his only opportunity for some specialization in a field of special concern to him, e.g. university education.

Educational Administration D is subtitled "Theory and Practice of Administration". The first strand examines the contributions of social psychology and group dynamics to an understanding of behaviour in organizational settings. Strand two examines some of the practical implications of these contributions for those working in educational organizations.

Dissertation requirements are unchanged.

It is anticipated that candidates progressing to the degree of Bachelor of Education will be required to do additional work to the field of Organization Theory.

EXTERNAL STUDIES

The division of the present courses into "foundation" and "professional" years illustrates the early belief that candidates for the diploma were likely to be external students. From 1959 to 1962 no courses were offered to either full-time or part-time students, but this was remedied from 1963. To date (June 1964) in spite of the many enquiries received, no full-time students have enrolled, although seven part-time students are receiving evening instruction at present.

The bulk of the candidates, then, have been and are likely to remain external students. The University of New England is very experienced in the instruction of external students, of which there are now well over 2,000 enrolled. The University's Department of External Studies is a purely administrative department which acts as a channel for communication between lecturer and student. Academic staff are appointed to the university on the understanding that they will teach external as well as internal students. There are thus no "special" lecturers for external students. It is a strict rule of the university that external students must come into residence for face to face contact with lecturers for certain periods during their courses.

The external Diploma in Educational Administration students fit into this general framework. (It is noteworthy, however, that in all other external courses, enrolment is restricted to residents of New South Wales.) Instruction is by means of "units", written material which is designed to guide the student's reading, present him with information not readily available in reference books, and assist him with his written exercises. "Supplementary" material is issued to supplement the units; this usually takes the form of reprints of journal articles and other materials, such as rating scales and organization charts.

This material is circulated at regular intervals throughout the year, and students "feed back" to their lecturers written exercises which may or may not grow out of the "unit" or "supplementary" material. At present five written exercises are required in connection with each of the old regulations foundation courses, four with each of the old regulations professional courses.

An overall timetable of the due dates of exercises is kept, and in an attempt to equate "external" teaching to the regularity of "internal" lectures, considerable importance is attached to the submission of exercises by the due dates. Students are, of course, encouraged to write to or call on their lecturers as often as they please. Further, they have access to a well-stocked library which is exclusively for the use of "externals", and exercises are set in such a manner as to require considerable use of library facilities.

Each year residential schools are arranged at Armidale (for foundation courses) and Sydney (for professional courses) during the May school vacation. The Armidale school is devoted in the main to lectures and tutorials of the traditional type. The Sydney school is largely devoted to a study of administration in organizations other than schools or universities. Organizations which have welcomed the students include the Australian Broadcasting Commission, Australian Gaslight Company, Australian Institute of Management, Balmain Hospital, Commonwealth Banking Corporation, Imperial Chemical Industries of Australia and New Zealand, the *Sydney Morning Herald*, Prince Henry Hospital, National Roads and Motorists' Association, David Jones Ltd., International Business Machines Ltd., New South Wales State Education Department, "Shore" School, Sydney Grammar School, and J. J. Cahill Memorial High School. The co-operation received from these organizations, their hospitality, and the frankness of their answers to the students' questions has been quite remarkable.

In addition to compulsory residential schools, students are requested to attend weekend schools which are held from time to time in centrally situated cities, normally Sydney.

THE FUTURE

From the introduction of the programme in 1959, an attempt has been made to evaluate systematically the success of the course (and its residential schools) by means of staff discussion and sampling of student opinion. As a result of this evaluation small changes have been made in the courses from time to time, an additional course has been introduced and several alterations have been made in the structure of residential schools.

A constant (and justifiable) complaint made by students is that the quantity and quality of the work required of them justifies the award of a qualification of higher status than that normally ascribed to a diploma. At the present time progression to the degree of Bachelor of Education requires one additional year of full-time or two additional years of part-time work.

The University of New England accepts a quota of twelve external (from outside the state) students and twenty-eight New South Wales students in each group enrolling for the first time. Many of the New South Wales students receive very tangible support from the state Education Department in the form of a fees warrant, assistance with travel, leave with pay to attend examinations and a grant towards the purchase of textbooks. The out-of-state students on the other hand, find themselves heavily out of pocket for fares, fees, and textbooks and usually must take leave without salary to attend residential schools during term time. It is to be hoped that other state Departments will sooner or later give some tangible encouragement to members of their staffs who are enthusiastic and capable enough to qualify for Australia's only "named" postgraduate qualification in the field of educational administration.

TEACHING AND RESEARCH IN EDUCATIONAL ADMINISTRATION

Adapted from a paper read at the first Seminar on Administrative Studies in the Research School of Social Sciences, Australian National University, Canberra, August 1963 and reprinted, by permission, from the *Journal of Educational Administration*, II no. 1 (May 1964), pp. 9-22.

THE SCHOOLS HAVE NOT PROGRESSED

The administrative revolution is only now beginning to influence the schools of Australia. A sixty-year old teacher, returning from abroad and visiting a public high school for the first time in forty years, would probably observe little to distinguish it as an administrative unit from the high school in which he taught in his youth.

If the visitor arrived at morning tea time he would not be surprised to observe that the headmaster and his deputy drink their tea in regal isolation, while the remainder of the staff retire to departmental staff rooms which appear to be distributed geographically in such a way as to inhibit any tendency towards that informal, institution-wide communication which such a large, complex organization would seem to demand.

If the teacher were a particularly tenacious visitor, and managed to visit the school regularly over a period of twelve months or so, he would probably not be surprised to observe many reminders of his youth: the attempt to put into operation a complex organization of over twelve hundred people without so much as a preliminary staff meeting; the chaotic line-up of parents, children, and newly appointed teachers outside the headmaster's office on the first day of term; the lack of comfortable facilities to put parents and other visitors at their ease; a marked lack of upward and downward communication in the hierarchical structure of the school; a reluctance to involve staff in decision making; and a tendency to look always to the central office of education before taking action—a general disinclination on the part of the head to test the limits of his authority.

In vain would the visitor scan the headmaster's shelves for a single book or journal devoted to educational administration—unless the publication were supplied *gratis* by the state. There would be little point in the visitor's looking for evidence of membership in the Australian Institute of Management or of completion of a disciplined university or other course in administration, for almost inevitably he would be disappointed.

THE ADMINISTRATOR-TEACHER DICHOTOMY

It seems clear that too many Australian schools are being administered by men and women who have rarely, if ever, thought seriously about the administrative process. As Simon[1] would say of them:

> They seldom deliberately set out to consider the ways in which the co-operative activities of groups are actually arranged, how the co-operation of groups could be made more effective and satisfying, what the requirements are for the continuance of the co-operative activity.

This is not to imply for one moment that headmasters are not interested in the efficiency of their schools. On the contrary, their own experience in schools, together with departmental regulations and traditions and the expectations of teachers, parents, and children, have produced a particular stereotyped form of behaviour and attitudes and have led to the adoption of particular role patterns which place considerable emphasis on the notion of efficiency.

The important point is that the stereotype of the Australian headmaster (except perhaps of the headmaster of an autonomous "Great Public School") does not include the concept of his being a real administrator, like the man who runs a hospital or an industrial plant. Traditionally—and this is a fact which in many ways is of immeasurable good to schools—Australian

[65]

headmasters have regarded themselves primarily as *teachers*. They have worked their way up "through the ranks", and their promotion has been as much dependent upon their ability as teachers as upon their likely ability to run a school in the departmental mould. There must be a great deal of sympathy extended towards this interest in teaching *per se*. Just as a surgeon demonstrates his greatest skill while operating, the teacher demonstrates his greatest skill while teaching. But the plain fact is that headmasters of large schools are no longer teachers. They are, or should be, *administrators*, and skill in teaching gives as little indication of one's prowess in running a school as skill in surgery gives of one's prowess in running a hospital.

Thus, the great enigma of school government today is that institutions which cry out for skilled administrators of wide vision are being run by men whose professional training and interests are not primarily in the field of administration at all.

At the state level, the picture is not very different. The departmental heads, like the headmasters above, are products of the system. Some of these officers are sent to courses such as those offered by the Administrative Staff College or the State Public Service Boards. Some of them travel abroad, but the effect of this obviously broadening experience is detracted from by the fact that travel tends to come too late in life and often consists of sporadic brief visits to a large number of educational institutions rather than a study in depth of a few institutions.

In contrast to headmasters, however, senior departmental officers do regard themselves as administrators and many of them do make an effort to read in the area of administration. It is only fair to point out that some of these officers do encourage headmasters who wish to enrol in courses in administration at university level, and in New South Wales they do issue a fees warrant for this purpose.

In spite of this growing interest in administration, the student of state offices can hardly avoid concluding that, with notable exceptions, the administrators there, protected from feedback which is critical of them as persons by a large, slow-moving machine and their position in the status hierarchy, are on the whole as unskilled at releasing the power of the group as are the headmasters below them.

Visitors to Australia, in company with many Australians, have often remarked upon the apparent emphasis on conformity, lack of adaptability, and hesitancy to experiment in our educational systems. The comments of Cannon,[2] Cunningham and Phillips,[3] Cramer,[4] Kandel,[5] McRae,[6] Butts,[7] Tibble,[8] and Jackson,[9] are well worth close scrutiny. Cramer, an American, probably summed up their arguments best when he wrote:

> The leaders of the state system are not opposed to new ideas. Progressive thought and experiments in education are attractive to them, in the abstract. Concretely, it is difficult to forget that everything they do is likely to set a precedent.[10]

The two Australians, Cunningham and Phillips, wrote:

> If it (a highly centralized system) does not actively provide in its machinery for penalties for departure from the beaten track it rarely provides any incentives to it.[11]

The above comments, written in the 1930's, are echoed in recent reports. The present author, for example, wrote to the Carnegie Corporation in 1959:

> In U.S. schools . . . that conformity and fear of creating precedent that plays such a large role in our decision making is much less noticeable . . .[12]

Clearly, our administrators of schools and school systems are circumscribed, perhaps unconsciously, by lack of contact with educational practices which are *different*, which offer *competition*, which actively encourage the use of *initiative* and *experiment*. These are dragons in the path of any educational reform. They are hardly likely to slither aside and let pass without suspicion any institution outside of the state system—including the University—which seeks to challenge the administrator to "slip the bonds of earth" and to reach beyond his particular state's administrator stereotype.

In some quarters—though surely not in the one in which we at present find ourselves—the necessity for any formal study of administration on the part of educators is seriously questioned.

It is pointed out that the "school of hard knocks" has produced some excellent administrators. To this argument it can only be replied that many alumni of S.O.H.K. have indeed distinguished themselves, but that they might well have distinguished themselves much earlier and much more often if they had been able to avoid a long period of trial and error learning. It is doubtful whether we can any longer afford to be as wasteful of our resources of material and personnel as we have been in the past. More than half a century ago we decided that teachers must be trained for a number of years before being permitted to teach. As pointed out in an earlier paper, while we no longer expect teachers to learn at the expense of their pupils, we apparently applaud the notion of administrators learning at the expense of both pupils and teachers.[13]

Today, education is really big business. The state of New South Wales alone spends more than $2,000,000 per week on public education. A typical high school enrols 1,200 children, employs 40 or 50 teachers and 4 or 5 non-professional staff, is divided into many departments, operates several banking accounts, has an annual payroll of perhaps $200,000 and occupies a plant whose capital cost might well be $1,000,000. The people are entitled to receive their tax-dollar's worth from this institution. Wastefulness, of financial or human resources, is as inexcusable as it is in any enterprise.

But the fiscal aspect of the school's operation is the least important. While it is true that an economist might calculate the money value of a complete high school education for one individual, or even for a whole nation, it is also true that schools do not exist primarily for their economic value to individuals and society.

THE SCHOOL IS A UNIQUE SOCIAL INSTITUTION

In a very real sense the school is a unique institution. It exists, above all, *for children*, the most precious of all the community's possessions. At the same time it exists for *society* in that it is the only institution specifically charged by our society to transmit that which we regard as best in our cultural heritage. Thus it is supposed to lead the child to accept the mores of the

[68]

society, but at the same time to develop in him independence and creativity, so its function becomes peculiarly one of socialization.

It is obvious to even the most unsophisticated observer that the aims and purposes of schools are not agreed upon by our society. We all know that the primary aim of business is profit; of a hospital, cure of the patient. But what is the primary aim of the school? All of the following are considered as legitimate primary aims in some quarters: to build character, to achieve results in examinations, to inculcate religious dogma, to prepare students for the university, to serve as an agency of social mobility, to examine critically the standards and values of the community, to prepare for citizenship, and so on. How many Australians, or, for that matter, Americans, would accept the assertion of Roald Campbell that

> Critical thinking is the highest purpose the school can serve . . . No other agency in our society, whether political, religious or economic, can appraise controversial issues with as little bias as can the school.[14]

Campbell's argument is sound, but practising administrators, both in his country and ours, have learnt to their cost that schools must be careful what they criticize! It is commonly asserted that the school should lead society, but the school that is too far ahead of society is quickly attacked. This is a growing hazard for administrators in a country where, in spite of Bush's argument that the authority of the teacher is not questioned by parents,[15] the rising level of education is breeding a more vocal and critical parent than Australia has previously experienced. Clearly, one treads carefully in an institution which does things *to* people, rather than *for* them.[16]

THE POWER OF THE GROUP IS NOT RELEASED

Rarely does one observe a school or school system in which the lessons, for example, of the Hawthorne experiments or of the Ohio State studies in leadership[17] are understood or consciously applied. For reasons which do not concern us here,

Australian educational administrators appear to be particularly uninterested in "releasing the power of the group".

This lack of interest represents a major social and financial loss to Australia. Schools, because of their unique staff structure, present an unparalleled opportunity for professional involvement. A typical Australian school staff is made up of teachers with a tertiary education extending from at least two to more than five years. All are likely to be in the top quartile so far as I.Q. is concerned. The great majority of them are likely to be committed to teaching as a life work.[18] None of them is a junior in the sense that shopgirls, waitresses, and trainees are juniors, for teaching is clearly an adult occupation. With a combination of high intelligence, tertiary education, professional commitment, and maturity, the school administrator is presented with a remarkable opportunity for sharing in decision making, for delegation of authority, for involvement in the enterprise. What an opportunity is presented for displaying initiative, breaking new ground, testing the limits of discretion! What an opportunity for releasing the power of the group! And how widely is the opportunity ignored!

Administrators in other fields would give much for the opportunity of working with such a professionally dominant group. Imagine a retail store staffed only by directors and buyers or a hospital without the complications introduced by the presence of large numbers of domestics, wardsmen, and kitchen hands—not to mention trainee nurses.

UNIVERSITY COURSES IN EDUCATIONAL ADMINISTRATION

When, in 1959, the University of New England set out with the Armidale Teachers' College to plan a postgraduate course in educational administration, the preliminary discussions ranged over most of the matters that have been raised in this paper. The number and ferocity of the dragons in the path were fully recognized.

The problem was: How do we challenge a man to look beyond the confines of his own system, to recognize the existence of a discipline of administration *qua* administration, to regard himself primarily as an administrator without harming his interest in teaching, to recognize the power in his hands to tap human resources, to appreciate the school's commitment to child and society?

The ways in which the University of New England and other Australian universities have attempted to meet these challenges is well documented. (See Chapter 5 of this volume.)

It is of interest to note, however, that much teaching in the area is peripheral to universities, although some departments of Adult Education or Extension arrange short courses or occasional lectures in the area. On the whole, it must be said, these are courses for the dilettante rather than the serious student. The same criticism might be levelled at the week-long courses sometimes offered by state teachers' colleges. Even when these are presented by challenging lecturers, the students rarely read books or prepare papers. Often, when taught by departmental officers, they deteriorate into a form of in-service induction to departmental stereotypes. This does not deny the value of some courses arranged by departmental officers, especially the residential courses in which non-departmental resource people are centrally involved. However, it is argued here, and the present author has argued this in detail elsewhere, that of all the institutions in our society, it is the university which is best suited, and indeed, is most likely, to act as the catalyst in administrative reform.

RESEARCH HAS MERELY SCRATCHED THE SURFACE

The dynamics of administration and organization are by no means fully understood in spite of the great strides taken by the social sciences in recent years. The nature of decision making is almost as great a mystery as ever it was. We have merely dabbled in the study of communication. So far as Australian education is concerned, no adequate theory of administration has been delineated; no study has been made of the flexibility and adaptability of schools; the economics of education is largely a closed book; no disciplined enquiry has been made of the effects of distance of schools from the central office; leadership behaviour has not been investigated; and so on.

[71]

There are vast uncharted areas which cry out for research. An obvious (and pressing) example is that of staff evaluation. In business there appears to be little question of the abilities required in management, nor does the assessment of competence seem a complicated process. Failure to produce profit results in a change in management. But the school makes no easily measurable profit, in spite of its rapidly rising costs, and systems of quality control and cost accounting are as out-of-place in the academic life of schools today as they would have been in the universities of mediaeval times. The problem has been put in a nutshell by the American Association of School Administrators:

> Many seeds planted in the hearts and minds of children during their early formative years do not come to fruition immediately. Appraising such fundamental changes in the lives of children cannot be made over a weekend as can the taking of an inventory in a hardware store.[19]

This question of teacher evaluation is of key importance in any educational system, but it is of supreme importance for the morale of teachers, and hence of children, in great centralized systems like those of the Australian states where teachers are promoted following inspection by state officers. In spite of the undoubted sincerity and enthusiasm of these officers, many of them would be the first to admit that their decisions are highly subjective and would be unlikely to stand up to an instrument measuring re-test reliability.

Teaching, like administration, is so much an interaction situation, its aims so diverse and numerous, its criteria of excellence so difficult to arrive at, that it might well be that an acceptable measuring instrument or process is unlikely to be developed in the foreseeable future. Certainly, we are making no great effort to arrive at such measures or processes.

The major problem is, of course, the setting up of criteria. Where are these to be found? In the syllabus? But it is widely agreed that schools do not exist merely to teach facts. In exam results? But are not examination marks themselves notoriously unreliable measures? In changed attitudes? But how could the attitudes engendered in the home and other social agencies be differentiated from those engendered in the schools? And so on, *ad infinitum*.

Nevertheless, it is not being too sanguine to hope that so long as there are administrators who assert, "Of course, our inspection system isn't perfect, but it does bring the best men to the top (look at me!)", there will be a group of thoroughly irritated and enquiring research workers who will challenge the validity of many of our common assumptions. Perhaps part of the answer will be found in the structured, broad approach taken in the Mort-Cornell Scale[20] or in the Growing Edge instrument.[21] A more rewarding approach, however, is likely to lie in the study of the behaviour of teachers, just as the Ohio State studies in the behaviour of leaders were able to determine, through the mass of common assumptions about leaders, that such behaviour is best defined in terms of two dimensions, Initiating Structure-in-Interaction and Consideration.[22]

A good example of the approach as applied to the behaviour of principals of schools was referred to in a previous chapter— the use of the "in-basket" technique in a study of the dimensions of administrative performance by Columbia Teachers' College and the Educational Testing Service.[23] There are exciting possibilities in this "action" technique. As Halpin pointed out when presenting his paradigm for research in administrative behaviour, a theory of educational administration must be predicated not only on the assumption that there is a discipline of administration *qua* administration that is worthy of study, but that greater strides will be made at this juncture if research efforts are focussed upon the *behaviour of administrators* rather than upon administrative behaviour or the totality referred to as administration.

Griffiths, for example, applies the same argument to the study of decision making. Gulick's POSDCORB (Planning, Organizing, Staffing, Directing, Co-ordinating, Reporting, Budgeting) he regards as merely descriptive of the total decision-making process. In other words, the decision-making process itself is regarded as sufficient to describe the nature of administration. Thus,

> The primary difference between a business organization and a school organization is not that one is a profit-making enterprise. The difference resides in the decision-making process. This is a difference of substance, not of form.[24]

Be this as it may, if a system of inspection is to be persevered with, some criteria of excellence are essential. Such criteria are usually dependent upon the theory of education which pervades the school—but where is there such a widely accepted, understood, or talked about theory underlying Australian education? As mentioned earlier, even the aims of the schools are by no means universally accepted. It is doubtful if most administrators outside of church schools, which have some clearly religious aims, and private schools, which have some clearly social aims, ever really entertain conscious thoughts on the matter. Yet, until the dialectics of a theory or theories of education, and hence of educational administration, emerge, the criteria of excellence must remain couched largely in terms of the "efficiency" which was so soundly rated by Kandel twenty-five years ago.

Here is an extraordinary opportunity for the Australian research worker to assist the administrator and teacher in identifying the dialectics upon which our theories will be built. As the American Association of School Administrators points out:[25]

> If professional education in general and school administration in particular are to be respected as disciplines to be learned and practised, it is time that there be drastic re-evaluation and re-organization of the knowledge and experience held to be essential to this discipline. The content belonging to this discipline should be clearly identified, organized and brought together in a logical manner rather than allowed to exist as an accretion of descriptive material and opinion.

Clearly, in Australia, as in the United States, we have a long way to go before these aims are achieved.

CONCLUSION

It is possible that this paper has overstated the case for the administrator at the expense of the teacher. When, at the beginning of the paper, the school administrator was described as being too concerned with teaching, it might well have been pointed out that there are many schools overseas, especially in North America, where the interest of the administrator is not at all directed towards teaching.

While the administration of universities has not been discussed in this paper, it is perhaps worthwhile noting that, rightly or wrongly, there is a growing feeling among Australian academics that the administrative staffs of universities are tending to depart from their traditional function of service to an academic community towards a managerial position where policy decisions which affect the academic life of the community are being made increasingly without reference to the traditional organs of university government. It is fair to say that at present Australian schoolteachers do not regard the administrators of their schools in quite this light. The reason for this might well be that Australian teachers have rarely been offered, nor have they asked for, an important role in school policy making.

It was with the dangers of the teacher-administrator dichotomy in mind that the University of New England's courses were designed to develop a concept of administration not as management, but as *education*. This was also the reason for the strong bias towards theory, principles, and research in the course structure.

The conclusion is unavoidable—that administration, like teaching, remains very much a pragmatic process, rich in opinion and folklore, but sadly lacking in scientific foundation and fact. Yet we have clearly arrived at a stage where we do, in fact, know a great deal—by no means enough, but a great deal—about *how* administrators behave, and how they *ought* to behave. What we do know deserves to be passed on to all administrators, whether or not they are students at a university. What we do not know deserves to be passed on too, in the interests of stimulating research and defeating the sham and cant so commonly associated with administrative practices.

At present we are plagued with a lack of serviceable language in administrative behaviour. In Chapter 1, I drew attention to Simon's claim that we "talk about organization in terms not unlike those used by a Ubangi medicine man to discuss disease".[26] Simon undoubtedly is correct. Is it too much to hope that one of the outcomes of this conference will be a pooling of resources in the hope that, at some future conference, definition of concepts will enable discussion to rise above the level of that accepted by the Ubangi medicine man?

SEVEN

THEORY AND PRACTICE IN EDUCATIONAL ADMINISTRATION

Adapted from a paper read at a conference on school administration, Faculty of Education, University of Queensland, Brisbane, 1964 and reprinted by permission from the *Journal of Educational Administration*, Vol. III, No. 1, May 1965. This paper develops in rather more detail a number of points regarding theory which have been raised in previous chapters. The author's heavy reliance on his U.S. colleagues, notably D. E. Griffiths and Andrew Halpin, is gratefully acknowledged.

> Theory is in the end . . . the most practical of all things, because the widening of the range of attention beyond nearby purpose and desire eventually results in the creation of wider and farther-reaching purposes, and enables us to make use of a much wider and deeper range of conditions and means than were expressed in the observation of primitive practical purposes.
>
> JOHN DEWEY

INTRODUCTION

So far as I have been able to ascertain, this is the first paper on the place of theory in the practice of educational administration to be read to a conference of school administrators in Australia. I confess that I face the task with considerable trepidation, for I am only too well aware that the word "theory" is anathema to good, solid practical administrators like yourselves.

We Australians, as Robin Boyd[1] has taken pains to point out, claim to have little use for theory. In this assertion we delude ourselves. As I shall show, the real distinction is not, as is commonly believed, between theory and practice, but between good theory and bad theory.

I hope in this paper to direct your attention to the frontiers of thought in administrative science. I use the expression "administrative science" advisedly, not because I reject entirely the notion that administration is an art (one of my favourite books adheres to this point of view)[2] but because I consider that a science of administration is at last within our grasp. I am by no means alone in this point of view, as is evidenced in the title of one of the most influential journals in our present area of interest—the *Administrative Science Quarterly*.

Little of the material included in this paper is my own. The basic work in this area has been done by a handful of men in the United States who have published a small collection of seminal books[3] which are likely to have a profound influence on our thinking during the next twenty years or so. So much have I taken from these scholars, especially Halpin and Griffiths, that at one stage I was tempted to pirate the title of Lord Wavell's famous anthology and call this talk "Other Men's Flowers". Perhaps this paper will persuade you to study the work of the above writers in their original writings.

I hope to present some of their ideas as guidelines for further reading and thought and to leave you with the task of evaluating them in the Australian setting. Figures 1–3 (pp. 90, 94, 95) show three models or paradigms which are concerned with administrative behaviour, and a case study at the end of this paper describes a rather tense relationship between principal Arthur Thompson and young Peter Bryant. I hope that you will try to assess the value of the paradigms in the light of the material presented in the case study.

A few months ago I suggested to the annual conference of the Queensland Teachers' Union that one of education's greatest needs is the development of a theory or theories of the teaching-learning process which will produce a set of principles on which action may be predicted and research may be based. Today my thesis is as deceptively simple: until such time as we arrive at a theory, or, more likely, theories which will enable us to understand, hypothesize about, and predict administrator behaviour, we shall remain in that pre-scientific trial-and-error, nakedly empirical state in which we see administration today.

THEORY AND PRACTICE ARE INSEPARABLE

As Griffiths has repeatedly stressed in his writings, the almost universally accepted dichotomy between theory and practice is founded on the untenable assumption that it is possible to make decisions and take action quite independently of our motives. We all know that our behaviour invariably serves the pursuit of some goal, and that our motives are shaped by certain explicit and implicit theories which we hold. We all know, too, that the making of a decision—any decision—involves some valuation on our part, some attempt to fit our decision into a supporting conceptual framework. Thus the decision whether a teacher should be reported for consistent unpunctuality may be taken on the basis of a belief, based on previous experience, that the rules of the employing authority are unnecessarily rigid where personal problems are concerned. You hypothesize that disciplinary action of this type will not lead to his reform.

Again, when you, an experienced principal of many years' standing, leaned across the breakfast table this morning and confided to a troubled colleague, "Take my tip. You do such-and-such. It's worked for me and everyone else I've known in thirty-five years with the Department . . ." you were theorizing. You were constructing theory in a manner which is in no way different from that adopted by an organic chemist: you expressed the results of your observations, and on the basis of your observations you predicted a future outcome.

In our schools we are surrounded by constant reminders of the close relationship between theory and practice. For example, when my father went to school his classroom was equipped with long desks screwed to the floor. When I first attended school nearly thirty years ago, we kindergarten children sat in movable individual tables and chairs, but when we moved up to the primary school we occupied dual desks which were securely screwed to the floor. The primary school attended by my children has no such thing as a fixed desk. Individual tables and chairs are provided and these are often placed in circles, or in small groups as well as in the traditional lines.

[79]

Why do you think that these changes have occurred? When we talk of a teacher-centred classroom or a child-centred classroom, are we not referring to a room in which the practices followed reflect certain theories of teaching and learning? I leave this simple example with you, though, of course, a host of similar questions could be asked about changes in school architecture, curriculum, teaching methods, and so on.

Clearly, the question of whether we should employ theory in our administrative behaviour is as meaningless as that of whether we should use motivation in our behaviour. The point is that all of us theorize, but that few of us develop *good* theory, that is, theory which reveals uniformities in the subject matter of the theory, which enables us to predict precisely in accordance with established criteria and provides guides to action which "work", or more rigidly, as defined by Griffiths[4] after Feigl, "a set of assumptions from which can be derived by purely logico-mathematical procedures a larger set of empirical laws".

Perhaps the alleged distinction between theory and practice is due to the obvious differences in the *use* made of theory by administrators and researchers. As Thompson[5] perceptively points out, while the administrator uses theory as a basis for deriving answers or approaches to specific situations, the scientist uses specific situations as a basis for arriving at improved theory. This does not mean, however, that the theory itself is different; only that it is put to different purposes.

WHAT IS THEORY?

While "theory" is used in a multitude of ways, unfortunately including the meaning "a set of oughts", we cannot here accept any definition of theory which is limited to mere observation, description, or classification of events. Theory here is regarded as a hypothesis which has undergone verification and which has potential

a) for explaining and predicting events, and

b) for the production of new knowledge.

Griffiths[6] helps us see where we are going by spelling out what a theory is *not*. It is not

a) *A personal affair.* Personal procedures developed by an individual administrator lack the breadth and depth and necessary consistency to be called a theory. Thus a theory transcends a personal manner of behaving.

b) *An idle dream.* Aimless speculation which lacks unification of concepts is not theory.

c) *A philosophy.* Philosophy is concerned with values and helps to indicate what an administrator *ought* to do. Models or theories of administration are concerned with what "is" rather than what "ought" to be. Science is concerned with a description of what *is*. While it is true that the administrator's behaviour will be influenced by values, these values are really variables applied to the model.

d) *A taxonomy.* A taxonomy is merely a classification of data according to some scheme of relationship. Taxonomies do not allow one to develop testable hypotheses from them as is possible under the formulation of my theory.

A good theory exists, according to the same author,[7] when there has been established a set of principles upon which action may be predicted. Such a theory would enable an administrator to make decisions with a good chance of being correct most of the time. The question of prediction is vital. In the physical sciences the object of the prediction (e.g. the gas described in Boyle's law) can do nothing about the prediction, while in the social sciences the object of the prediction (a person) is inextricably woven with it, often knows what the prediction is, and can do something about it.

Theory, whether in the physical or social sciences, always begins with observations. To be of any value the observations must be presented in the form of *facts*. As Johnson[8] points out,

> A fact is necessarily incomplete, it changes, it is a personal affair, and its usefulness depends on the degree to which others agree with you concerning it.

The implications of this are

a) that observers should be as little involved in the events being reported as possible, in order to ensure objective descriptions, and

b) that reports of observations must be couched in clear, understandable language and described in enough detail to lead
the reader to understand the methods used and the observation which was made.

The achievement of the latter criterion is closely allied to the
whole notion of *concept* development. This is a semantic problem.
Confusion is the inevitable result, unless concepts mean the
same thing to all workers in the field. As Simon[9] points out,
these concepts, to be scientifically useful, must be operational,
i.e. their meanings must correspond to empirically observable
facts or situations. Consider, for example, our loose use of what
have become everyday words like administration, supervision,
decentralization, training, instruction, teaching. How many of
these have been defined operationally to your knowledge?

Many workers interested in the development of theory have
been deterred from going deeply into the problem because they
have been overcome by the sheer mass of detail which appears
to be essential if the theory is to have any value. They do not
realize that, even in the physical sciences, many important
factors are left out of a theory in its formulation. For example,
friction is omitted from the laws of motion. If friction had been
left in, no theory of motion would have been possible.

"Practical" men often criticize theories as being emasculated
and hence absurd. But Griffiths[10] points out that theory must
always leave something out. It should be evaluated on the basis
of *what is in*, rather than what is left out. "A theory may be the
truth, but not the whole truth."

THE USES OF THEORY

An obvious use is as a guide to new knowledge. Since a theory
is by its nature both deductive and inductive, it is possible to
say: "If such and such is true, then such and such must follow."
Alternatively it should be possible to test a theory by saying:
"If such and such happens, then such and such must be true."
The discovery of the planet Neptune, following theoretical
deductions based on the observation of a periodic irregularity
in the path of Uranus, is an excellent example of theory producing new knowledge.

As a guide to research, it is essential. As Dallenbach[11] points out: "Doing something without a theory is not a scientific experiment. It is mere busy work."

In administration, however, theory's main place is as a guide to action. Griffiths presents a cogent analogy from the field of medicine:

> Unless a theory can provide guidance for the administrator when he needs to act, it is a poor theory indeed. The educational administrator should be able to use theory in much the same way as a practising doctor should be able to use the theory developed by researchers in biological laboratories. The doctor does not necessarily know the theory of, for instance, mold growth, to be able to use penicillin to cure a streptococcus infection; yet he would be a very poor doctor if he did not use penicillin. In like manner, the educational administrator should be able to look to administrative theory for guidance in, for instance, the solution of a problem of faculty morale.

Such an assertion is likely to be met with scorn in some quarters. Educational Administration has been based on empirical foundations; it has evolved, as Marland[12] puts it,

> as a quasi-professional apprenticeship or folklore with techniques and processes handed down from one generation to another through the trial and error, hard-knock pattern.

Administrators are the practical "get-the-job-done" men who know what will work and what will not, because they have tried the solutions available, or they know good men who have. Marland, himself a practising school superintendent, compares the present-day situation in flight with that of the 1920's, when the bush pilot flew his aeroplane "by the seat of his pants". For the time, S.O.P. flying was successful, right, and good for the aircraft. In any case there was little else upon which to rely. Now, however,

> The bush pilot... finds himself in the pilot's chair of a monstrous flying machine of untold power and dimensions. The social scientist tells us that there are buttons to push, levers to adjust, gauges to watch, beacons to reckon and

codes to decipher. He tells us that one cannot fly this craft by the seat of the pants, but that certain buttons and levers, when actuated, produce specific and predictable results in the performance and posture of the craft.

Marland's rather high-flown analogy may be contrasted with the rather more restrained argument of Getzels,[13] who presents a convincing case based on the difference between an itinerary and a relational map. He rejects the attitude towards school administration as a problem in human engineering, as a practical, prescription-centred viewpoint which depends for guidance upon a previously tested set of directions, or an *itinerary*. He argues that the focus of effort must be not on prescriptions but on theories; not on simple directions, but on complex relationships; not on specific itineraries, but on relational *maps*.

The itinerary approach is seductively practical: the ready-made solutions and simple prescriptions appeal so much to common sense. But is it as practical as it seems? Just how many administrative problems are simple, straightforward problems? What happens when your itinerary becomes impracticable—when a bridge has been washed away or your car will not climb a hill? Surely such a situation requires a map showing alternative routes to suit the exigencies of each situation. Getzels asserts:

> To be sure, theories without practices, like maps without routes, may be empty, but practices without theories, like routes without maps, are *blind* . . . So-called practical principles cannot be either meaningfully formulated or effectively applied outside a supporting conceptual framework.[14]

This, incidentally, is a problem which the lecturers responsible for the University of New England's courses in educational administration are constantly meeting—the demand by students for practical advice, the "good guts", itineraries—when all that we can do—indeed, intend to do—is to provide maps.

As we shall see later, each administrative situation is unique —it depends upon an infinite number of variables associated with the persons and institutions involved. To expect someone who is not acquainted with the dynamics of the situation to provide solution A to problem A is hopeless indeed. This is why authors of case studies do not provide solutions to the problems they raise: every man must be his own saviour, whether he flies by the seat of his pants or not.

THEORY CONSTRUCTION

Most writers who are interested in theory, including Griffiths, refer to Homans' classic work of 1950, *The Human Group*.[15] Homans sets out the following set of notes for theory building:

1. Look first at the obvious, the familiar, the common. In a science that has not established its foundations, these are the things that best repay study.
2. State the hypothesis in its full generality. Science is an economy of thought only if its hypotheses sum up in a simple form a large number of facts.
3. Talk about one thing at a time. That is, in choosing your words (or, more pedantically, concepts) see that they refer not to several classes of fact at the same time, but to one and one only. Corollary: Once you have chosen your words, always use the same words when referring to the same things.
4. Cut down as far as you dare the number of things you are talking about. "As few as you may: as many as you must" is the rule governing the number of classes of fact you take into account.
5. Once you have started to talk, do not stop until you are finished. That is, describe systematically the relationships between the facts designated by your words.
6. Recognize that your analysis must be abstract, because it deals with only a few elements of the concrete situation. Admit the dangers of abstraction, especially when action is required, but do not be afraid of abstraction.

Using these rules as a guide Griffiths[16] sets out to illustrate the steps to be followed in developing a theory of administrative behaviour:

1. A *description* of administrative behaviour in one situation. Social behaviour must begin with facts of this sort—a statement of an observation made by an observer who does

not, by his presence, change the situation, and who can view what happens with objectivity.

2. A *definition* of certain basic concepts.

Once the description is studied it becomes obvious that there are certain basic concepts that need refinement and definition. This is necessary so that the concept will be used in exactly the same way in later instances.

3. A more *general statement* which is descriptive of average behaviour in a limited number of situations.

Theory is not built upon isolated instances of behaviour; it is concerned with the nonchance variations in behaviour. In other words a theory of administrative behaviour should deal with the common or general types of behaviour.

4. A statement of one or more *hypotheses*.

At this stage it is necessary to state some testable hypotheses. They should be stated in the form of "if—then" statements.

5. An *evaluation* and *reconstruction* of the hypotheses in accordance with later observations.

The hypotheses must be rigorously tested and, if necessary, revised to take into account the new insights gained in the testing process.

6. The statement of *principles*.

The final step is the statement of a principle or set of principles which are general statements of such a nature as to enable a person to make an accurate prediction of administrative behaviour.

Shortly we shall look at two models, the first of which is described as providing a step *towards* a theory, the second as a hypothetico-deductive theory in its own right. At the conclusion of this paper I should like you to examine these models and Griffith's theory as building steps in the light of the case study on Peter Bryant. I hasten to explain that I did not write the case for this purpose. It was written to introduce a discussion on professional ethics at a headmasters' meeting in Armidale. It was designed, if I remember correctly, with "oughts" in mind, but on re-reading it seems to be just as suitable for a discussion of "is's".

After reading the case you might attempt to *describe* Arthur Thompson's behaviour, *define* any concepts which are likely to prove troublesome, arrive at a *general statement* which describes average behaviour in a number of situations (not just this head in this school), set up one or more testable *hypotheses* in the "if—then" pattern, suggest ways to *evaluate* and *reconstruct* them in the light of your observation, and state one or more *principles*.

THE SEARCH FOR THEORY

It is crucial that at this point of the discussion we recognize that no theory is likely to be *the* theory. As Halpin[17] puts it,

> There is more than one way to the kingdom of knowledge. Each gate opens upon a different vista but no one vista exhausts the realm of "reality"—whatever that may be.

It is also crucial that we recognize, with Getzels,[18] that there is nothing to be gained from being afraid of theory. A theory can be wrong and still lead to progress. This has been demonstrated repeatedly in physics, for example, yet the rejected theories were not a waste of time. Thus, "Explicit theory—even *wrong* explicit theory—is better than implicit theory or no theory at all".

Attempts to arrive at theory in educational administration are of recent origin. However, essays at a systematic definition of administration are much older, probably as old as the fifteenth century, and certainly the eighteenth century, in which the German Cameralists were writing extensively.

The attempt to apply the scientific method to all aspects of organization is a twentieth century phenomenon. Fayol[19] in France, Urwick[20] in England, Mary Parker Follett,[21] Gulick,[22] Tead,[23] and Mayo[24] (to name but a few) in America have contributed a vast store of ideas and information on the administrative process.

The first attempt at formulating a comprehensive theory in the hypothetico-deductive sense as distinct from taxonomies was presented by the eminently successful practitioner, Barnard[25] in his *Functions of the Executive*, published in 1938. Barnard regarded formal organization as the "concrete social

[87]

process by which social action is largely accomplished". He sought to formulate a conceptual framework for the study of organization, which he defined as "an impersonal system of co-ordinated human beings".

Simon's *Administrative Behavior*,[26] with its emphasis upon decision making as the core of the administrative process, has exerted a considerable influence in recent years. Argyris[27] has presented a theory which is aimed at revealing an understanding of the mechanism by which the individual actualizes himself through the organization and simultaneously the organization actualizes itself through the individual.

The theorists in educational administration are thinking along lines parallel to those in other spheres of administration. Griffiths[28] developed a model which conceived of administration as decision making. He argued that theory must deal with the *substance* of administration, not its *form*, and that all functions of administration can best be interpreted in terms of the decision making process.

Hemphill[29] proposed a theory of administration as problem solving, based on the important work on leader behaviour carried out at Ohio State University during the 1950's. He argued that leader behaviour could be thought of in terms of two dimensions—consideration and initiating structure-in-interaction.

Guba[30] and Getzels[31] have presented an influential theory which views administration as a social process. Administration is conceived of "*structurally* as the hierarchy of subordinate-superordinate relationships within a social system. *Functionally* this hierarchy of relationships is the locus for allocating and integrating roles and facilities in order to achieve the goals of the social system."

We shall return to this model later.

In the past, theorists in educational administration have tended to draw their inspiration from theorists in other "adjectival" administrations. There are signs, however, that the theorists in educational administration are now pointing the way to others, as Griffiths'[32] recent paradigm for the development of theory demonstrates. There have, too, been some important research projects associated with certain theories, notably the simulated Whitman School project reported in Hemphill's *Administrative Performance and Personality*.[33] Such theorizing and researching may be expected to grow in scope and insight with the further development of the University Council for Educational Administration[34] both as a national and an international body.

HALPIN'S PARADIGM

Perhaps we should all now consult Halpin's Paradigm.[35] Here is a model which is not intended as a theory, but which clearly has implications for research in administrator behaviour: it is *"one* way of thinking about research in administration that may accelerate the development of a useful theory".

I shall attempt to present Halpin's argument in his own terms wherever possible.

Administration in any sphere involves a minimum of four components:

1. The task
2. The formal organization
3. The work group
4. The leader.

Each of these terms is defined by Halpin. The task is the purpose or mission of the organization as defined by observers of the organization proper. Thus the task of school X is defined by public consensus, the State Department of Education, and by the policies of the local Board of Education.

An organization is defined as "a social group whose members are differentiated as to their responsibility for accomplishing the group's task". Halpin recognizes the existence of both a formal and an informal organization, whose networks do not always coincide. There are thus two fundamental sets of variables which define the operations of an organized group. These are:

1. Variables which define formal organization: i.e.,
   a) responsibility variables (the work one is expected to do);
   b) formal interaction variables (the persons with whom one is expected to work).

[89]

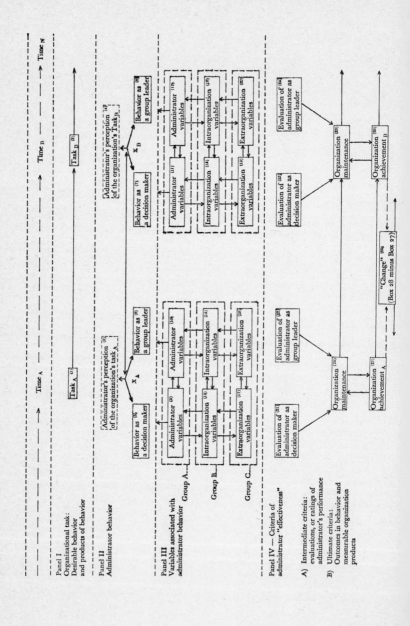

2. Variables which define informal organization: i.e.,
   a) work performance variables (the tasks one actually performs);
   b) informal interaction variables (the persons with whom one actually works).

The *work group* is comprised of individuals chosen to fill positions specified by the formal organization.

The *leader* is one member of the organization formally charged with the responsibility for the organization's accomplishment.

The paradigm is predicated upon three basic assumptions about administrator behaviour in education and upon two methodological assumptions. The behavioural assumptions are:

1. The public school organization is constituted for a purpose and this purpose can be stated in terms of "desired" outcomes—either "desirable" behaviour or "desirable" products of behaviour. These outcomes constitute the organization task.
2. The individuals who compose the organization are engaged in continuous problem solving in their effort to accomplish this task.
3. The administrator is the formally designated leader of the organization. Three areas of behaviour are of special importance:
   a) his perception of the organization's task;
   b) his behaviour as a decision-maker;
   c) his behaviour as a group leader *vis-à-vis* his own immediate work group.

The two methodological assumptions are:

1. it is desirable to confine the enquiry to concepts that have definable referents in behaviour or in the products of behaviour;
2. it is important to discriminate between *descriptions* of behaviour and *evaluations* of behaviour.

Panel I refers to the organization's task. Because behaviour takes place through *time* the time line is extended horizontally. The task is expressed by outside observers as a set of "ideal" objectives that specify what the organization *ought* to do rather than what it does, i.e., in terms of changes that the organization seeks to induce either in behaviour or in the products of behaviour. Although there is likely to be little change in tasks in a stable organization, the paradigm provides for some change in tasks, i.e. from Task A to Task B.

Panel II refers to administrative behaviour in terms of the three areas of behaviour indicated above. Through his perception of the task the leader defines the organization's problems. These would have to be expressed in *behavioural* terms, not in clichés and slogans. It should be clearly noted that the leader's *perception* of the task is a different thing from the task in Panel I. His perception defines the problem and his behaviour both as a decision maker and as a group leader depends upon this perception.

For the moment let us omit Panel III.

Panel IV is concerned with criteria of administrator effectiveness. The ultimate criteria of administrator "effectiveness" should be expressed in terms of organization achievement, i.e. in respect to changes in the organization's accomplishments that can be attributed to the behaviour of the administrator. This can be measured by the differences between the organization's achievements at Time A and Time B in respect to whatever products are specified.

Thus, although the Task may be stated in "oughts", the achievement must be measured in terms of "is's". For example, the aims of improving "citizenship" can only be measured in terms of specific dimensions of *behaviour* which can be reliably observed and reported upon. If this requirement is not satisfied, it is impossible to know whether or not the administrator has accomplished the organization's task. Research will make little progress until the task and the organizational outcomes are stated in the same language.

Included in "ultimate criteria" are changes in organization maintenance as well as organization achievement. For example, a change in "morale" (organization maintenance) does not necessarily guarantee a corresponding change in the organization's achievement.

The most crucial research task in educational administration is to prove that the various intermediate criteria of administrator "effectiveness" now used so glibly are, in fact, significantly corrclated with the changes in the organization's achievement.

Panel III illustrates the variables which affect the relationship between the administrator behaviour variables in Panel II and the "effectiveness" criteria of Panel IV. These have been divided into three broad groups:

a) *Administrator variables*

Attributes and characteristics of the administrator that can be measured apart from his membership of the organization, e.g. age, intelligence, academic background, experience, personality characteristics, and so on. The two vertical channels are separated so as to point to the need for research on the extent to which skills that contribute to good decision making also contribute to good group leadership.

b) *Intraorganization variables*

These refer to measurable characteristics of the organization's administrative structure, of the group as a group, and of the group members other than the leader.

c) *Extraorganization variables*

These refer to variables outside the formal organization, such as community mores, population increases, racial conflicts, and the like.

The total paradigm

Research efforts to date have largely focussed upon Panel III *within* the panel, and upon the relationship between administrator variables and intermediate criteria of administrator effectiveness, without either going through Panel II or following through from Panel IVA to IVB to demonstrate the relationship between evaluations of the administrator and objective criteria of the organization's accomplishments.

What is now needed is a much greater emphasis on research relevant to Panels II and IV.

This paradigm should be of considerable interest to Australian educators who, in state schools at least, are handed a syllabus which sets out certain objectives and goals and are then inspected to see how effectively these objectives and goals have been achieved. I hope that some of you after further reading of

[93]

Halpin will interpret this paradigm for Queensland conditions and will suggest areas of research which may be necessary to classify our current practices and beliefs.

Halpin's paradigm presented a crude, heuristic approach towards the development of a theory of educational administration. Let us now turn to Getzels' paradigm,[36] which has been presented as a *theory* in its own right; and attempt to describe it in his own words wherever possible.

It derives from the assumption that the school is a social system. A social system involves two classes of phenomena:

a) the institutions with certain roles and expectations that will fulfil the goals of the system

b) the individuals with certain personalities and need-dispositions whose observed interactions we call social behaviour.

Behaviour associated with institution, role, and expectation is referred to as the normative or *nomothetic* dimension of activity

(Nomothetic dimension)

Institution ⟶ Role ⟶ Expectations

Social system

Observed behaviour

Individual ⟶ Personality ⟶ Need-disposition

(Idiographic dimension)

in a social system; that associated with an individual, personality, and need-disposition is referred to as the personal or *idiographic* dimension of the social system.

Getzels argues that to understand the nature of observed behaviour, and to be able to predict and control it, we must understand the nature and relationship of these elements.

Institutions are agencies which carry out certain routinized tasks for the social system as a whole. The most important analytic units of an institution are *roles*, which may be defined in terms of *expectations*, i.e. of the rights, privileges, and obligations to which any incumbent of the role must adhere. Roles are *complementary*, i.e. each role derives its definition and meaning from other related roles; for example the role of leader cannot be understood except in relation to the role of follower.

Roles, however, are implemented by living individuals, all of whom differ in some respects; thus, to understand administrative behaviour, we must know the nature of the individuals inhabiting the roles and reacting to the expectations.

Personality is referred to as the dynamic organization within the individual of those need-dispositions that govern his unique reactions to the environment and to expectations of his environment. The central analytic elements of personality are need-dispositions.

Thus, to understand the behaviour and interaction of specific role-incumbents in specific institutions, he must know both the role expectations and the need-dispositions.

The theory is clearly illustrated in the diagram (see p. 94).

The proportion of role and personality factors determining behaviour will vary with the specific act, the specific role, and

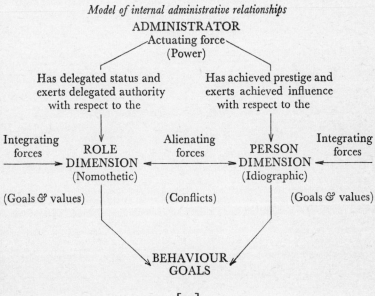

Model of internal administrative relationships

ADMINISTRATOR
Actuating force
(Power)

Has delegated status and exerts delegated authority with respect to the

Has achieved prestige and exerts achieved influence with respect to the

Integrating forces

ROLE DIMENSION (Nomothetic)

Alienating forces

PERSON DIMENSION (Idiographic)

Integrating forces

(Goals & values)

(Conflicts)

(Goals & values)

BEHAVIOUR GOALS

[95]

the specific personality involved. Behaviour can thus be described as either predominantly role-relevant (e.g. behaviour during a staff meeting) or personality relevant (e.g. choosing colours for walls of a new assembly hall).

Guba[37] has developed the socio-psychological map on page 95 into what he calls a "working model" or a theory of reality which we are trying to understand, predict, and control. The model requires four elements:

1. *Behavioural determinants.* Unless we wish to take the view that behaviour is produced in a completely random way (in which case the conception of a science of behaviour would be absurd) we need to assume for the sake of model building that there exist certain classes or categories of what might be called "determinants" or perceptions of behaviour.
2. *Alienating forces.* Where several sets of behavioural determinants may exist simultaneously, it seems inevitable that, on occasion, behavioural determinants will be in conflict concerning the nature of the behaviour to be displayed.
3. *Integrating forces.* Where alienating forces exist, disruption of the system is the inevitable result unless some other opposing system of forces is operative.
4. *Actuating forces.* There is clearly some compelling or actuating force which the subject finds impossible to resist and which can require certain behaviour of him.

Now, the science of administration is obviously a science of managing behaviour. The behavioural determinants are the nomothetic and idiographic dimensions. The task of the administrator is that of mediating between these two sets of behaviour-eliciting forces so as to produce behaviour which is at once organizationally useful and individually satisfying. Action which will lead to such behaviour on the part of personnel is the highest expression of the administrator's art.

The alienating forces may be seen as specific points of divergence between or within the nomothetic and idiographic dimensions. For example, the role elements may be inconsistently defined, or defined in such a way as to require behaviours which are mutually exclusive: e.g. the principal who is cast in the role of disciplinarian and counsellor or—dare I mention it—

the inspector who is cast in the role of both adviser and assessor. Further, personal elements may be inconsistent—a state which in its extreme form is described as schizophrenia. An additional tension lies in the existence of the square peg in the round hole: i.e. the nomothetic and idiographic elements are inconsistent.

It is important to notice, however, that conflict is probably normal within an organization, and while we try to avoid it, it is nonetheless true that it serves a major institutional function in causing change to occur.

While alienating forces lie in wait to pester the administrator, he has at his disposal integrating forces which are his allies. These reside in the role incumbents themselves: for example, in the need for socially constructive activity, or sharing in cultural values, a deep commitment to such organizational goals as the education of young children. It goes without saying that the alert administrator seeks to understand the dynamics of such forces in his organization.

The last category—the actuating force which makes the system go—lies in the *power* of the administrator himself. It is important to notice, however, that power is inherent in *both* the idiographic and the nomothetic dimensions. In terms of the nomothetic dimension the administrator has prestige and creates influence; in terms of the idiographic dimension prestige and influence must be achieved individually. This is what we mean when we say that it is individual behaviour which makes authority effective.

Let us now look at Guba's model.

The administrator is attempting to elicit human behaviour consistent with the fulfilment of certain goals. The flow of the arrows indicates that both the role and the person must be taken into account.

The force implied by the arrows flowing down consists of his power, which is clearly of two kinds. On the role dimension his status is tied to his office. Here he defines roles, applies rewards or punishments, and makes decisions. Here his power is *delegated*.

On the person dimension, status is *achieved*: he develops his prestige and influence on the basis of merit.

[97]

It is worthwhile noting that the administrator without influence in *both* of these dimensions is half powerless. The martinet who rules through the role dimension alone is indeed a pitiful sight—but no more so than the mistakenly "democratic" leader who abdicates his delegated responsibility and who tries to work through the idiographic dimension alone.

The inevitable gap between the role and person dimensions—the producer of alienation—is clearly shown on the diagram. This alienation occurs inevitably whenever there is a staff of more than one person and thus is the *usual* state for an organization.

The integrating forces which hold an organization together are also clearly shown. The administrator who can sense common commitments and values, or who can develop them when none exist, enlists a powerful ally without whose aid the task of maintaining an integrated organization is almost impossibly difficult.[38]

This diagram sums up much of what we know today. It also highlights our points of weakness, for there are many "soft" spots. Nonetheless it provides us with an entry to the still elusive frontiers of administrative science.

As we have seen, this is but one theory—a promising theory it is true—among many.

The great task of science has been, as Griffiths[39] so persuasively puts it, to impose *order* upon the universe.

> Kepler's laws, for instance, impose a set of relationships upon the planets of the solar system. Within the framework of laws, the motions of the planets make sense, their positions can be predicted, and order is apparent to all who care to look. This is the great task of theory in the field of educational administration. Within a set of principles, yet to be formulated, it will be possible to predict the behaviour of individuals within the organizational framework and it will be possible to make decisions that will result in a more efficient and effective enterprise. Research will have more meaning because it will be directed toward the solution of problems, have clear definitions and will contribute to the whole con-

cept of administration. It will be more easily understood because it will use concepts that have the same meaning to all in the profession.

Is Griffiths in his educational dotage? He uses the history of chemistry as an analogy, and cites the arguments of Cassirer:

Chemistry entered on the highway of science much later than physics, but it was not lack of new empirical evidence which obstructed the progress of chemical thought. The alchemists possessed an outstanding talent for observation. When, however, they began to describe their observations, they had no instrument of description except a half mythical language, full of obscure and ill-defined terms. They spoke in metaphors and allegories, not in scientific concepts. It was not until the time of Lavoisier that chemistry learned to speak a quantitative language, and when Dalton discovered his law of equivalent or multiple proportions a new way was opened to chemistry. Yet it was only with the discovery of the periodic system of the elements that chemistry acquired a new mathematical and deductive structure.

Griffiths asserts that today we live in an age of educational alchemy. Who dares challenge him?

PETER BRYANT LACKS COMMON SENSE

Arthur Thompson, Principal of Wright Street Public School, parked his car under a convenient peppercorn tree which stood near the boundary of the playground and strode into his office. It was 8.15 a.m., and only two or three children were playing around the buildings. Arthur looked forward to at least an uninterrupted half-hour in which to deal with accumulated mail.

He had just sat down at his typewriter when Mrs. Richards, the cleaner, knocked on the door. "Oh, hello, Mrs. Richards. How are you this morning?"

"Good thanks," replied the cleaner. "Mr. Thompson, come and have a look at Mr. Bryant's room. It's in a terrible mess again, and I don't know where to start."

Arthur followed her along the corridor to a Fourth class room and looked around quickly. Mrs. Richards' complaint was justified. There were scraps of paper on the floor, books

[99]

BELMONT COLLEGE LIBRARY

hanging haphazardly from below desks. These, like the ink-marked desks and pictures askew, were part of the normal scene in Bryant's room. But this time he had gone too far. On the teacher's table stood an ash tray piled high with cigarette butts, a half-drunk cup of coffee and some crusts in a piece of waxed paper. Rats had visited the table during the night.

"It's not my job to clean up after his meals," said Mrs. Richards. "Anyway, what would the union say?"

"But surely you cleaned the room yesterday afternoon."

"No, Mr. Thompson. Mr. Bryant wouldn't let me come in. He said he had a lot of work to do and that he didn't want to be disturbed. He said he'd probably stay on until tea-time. I asked him if I could just run the broom over the floor but he told me that the room wasn't really dirty, and to leave it until morning."

"Has this happened before?"

"Oh, often. There's usually been quite a mess to clean up, but never one as bad as this."

"It's disgusting. Well, see what you can do with it just this once more, Mrs. Richards. I'm sure it won't happen again," said Arthur grimly.

He strode into his office and shut the door. "Blast Bryant! Why is it always Bryant?" He attacked his typewriter.

At nine o'clock Arthur visited the staff room for his regular morning five-minute chat with members of staff who were not on playground duty or busy in their classrooms. Peter Bryant was sitting in a sunny corner, leisurely smoking a cigarette. He started when Arthur came in the door. "Good Lord. Nine already! I'm on playground duty."

"Oh, Peter, there are a few things I'd like you to do for me in a hurry. Would someone else go out to the playground? Peter will repay you later."

When Marie Snell stood up to go out Arthur asked Bryant to accompany him to the office. Peter Bryant sat down, lit up a cigarette without asking permission, and waited for Arthur to begin.

Arthur hesitated. He was not sure how to approach Bryant. From his observations in the classroom and in the playground he was convinced that Bryant had the makings of a good teacher. He appeared to try hard. Certainly his lessons and programme seemed to be carefully planned: and there was no doubt about his interest in the four-seven football team. On the other hand, his class was often unruly, and progress in most subjects was far from satisfactory. But he lacked common sense. He was constantly saying and doing things which irritated others. In his five years of teaching he had been in three schools. His first appointment had been to a small school where he had alienated all of the parents. The principal of the second school hastened to pass him on to another when his tardy and careless habits became obvious. The report written by his inspector had suggested that Mr. Bryant should seriously consider an occupation other than teaching. It was tacitly agreed that Peter was very much "on probation" in Arthur Thompson's school. Arthur was convinced of Peter's underlying worth and had avoided disciplining him, even when he felt that the interests of the children were endangered, in the hope that he would find his own feet.

"Look, Peter, Mrs. Richards took me along to see your room this morning. It was a disgusting mess."

"What's the state of the room got to do with her? She's paid to clean it, isn't she?"

"Yes, that's so. But it's a bit over the odds to expect her to clean up after your meal isn't it?"

"I worked back late last night. I knew you would want everything just right, with your special inspection coming up."

"That's a bit beside the point, isn't it?"

"I don't think so. Schools are not for cleaners. They're for teachers . . ."

"For children, I think," snapped Arthur. "Now for goodness sake try to show some common sense. A clean and tidy room is just as important for the kids as a clean and tidy notebook. You know as well as I do that the real test of your fitness to teach is being conducted in this school. I haven't spoken to you before, though goodness knows there were plenty of times when I should have done so."

Peter Bryant seemed chastened. "All right, Mr. Thompson; I'll do my best."

Arthur looked sorrowfully at the unfinished letter in his typewriter and left to teach his own class.

At morning recess Arthur's deputy, Bob Somers, joined him for their traditional morning cup of tea. "What did young Bryant say to Mrs. Richards this morning, Arthur? All I heard was a sarcastic 'Thanks very much!' when he came out of your room."

"Did he say that? I thought he left me a chastened young man. We'll have to watch him."

Bob Somers looked uncomfortable. "As a matter of fact there are a couple of things about Peter Bryant I should have mentioned to you earlier. We both know that his class is a shambles. And at the golf club a month or so ago, I heard that he was 'running you down' at the top of his voice to a crowd of his mates in the public bar of the 'Imperial'. And only yesterday I heard a couple of members of the anti-fluoridation league saying that they would report him if he continued to criticize them in class."

Arthur was staggered. "Why on earth didn't you tell me about the fluoridation business straight away? I'm not worried about his antics in the pub: it's every man's right to criticize his boss. But the fluoridation issue is another matter. Who told you about it?"

"Old Jacob Saunders. I didn't see any point in carrying tales. It's part of my job to protect you from petty details, isn't it? There's been no official complaint, and there's no harm done."

"This is hardly a petty issue. Old Saunders is sure to cause trouble, even if only at the P. and C. meeting. I'd better have a word with Bryant before we *do* hear something official."

Arthur once again called Bryant out of the staff room and asked him to go to his office. As succintly as possible, Arthur told Bryant what he had heard.

Peter Bryant seemed very upset. "What's wrong with taking sides on an issue like this? You know as well as I do that fluoridation of water supplies is strongly recommended by dentists and scientists."

"Of course I do; but the argument is a hot one just now. Why do you pick on our most controversial issue for discussion?"

"But I thought schools were the very places where controversial issues *should* be discussed. Do you mean we should only discuss events that are past, or that don't affect us directly? The syllabus says . . ."

"I don't care what the syllabus says. Use your brains! You'll get yourself—and me, too—in trouble over this. Have you tried to give both sides—pro and con?"

"Yes, of course. Very objectively, too."

"Thank goodness for that . . . There's the bell. We'll talk about this again later on . . ."

"Oh, Mr. Thompson, *please* don't come and pull me out of the staff room every time you want to see me. The others will think I'm being treated like an irresponsible kid."

Peter walked out of the office towards the assembly area.

At tea-time that evening Arthur could not resist the temptation to broach the topic of fluoridation with his daughter, Jill, whose best friend was in Peter Bryant's class. Jill was full of ideas on the subject. "Mr. Bryant says that people who don't want fluoride in the water are 'crackpots'," she volunteered. "He says they are like witches in the olden days. I think so, too. Don't you, daddy? I want to grow up with strong white teeth like Mr. Bryant's."

Arthur did not reply. He was determined to confront Bryant with his new information next morning.

After tea the phone rang. It was Jacob Saunders. "Arthur? You weren't at Rotary last Tuesday . . . Arthur, that young Bryant is stirring up trouble. He's been making all kinds of accusations against the anti-fluoridation league. The league is pretty upset about it. John Marley wanted to write to the Minister of Education, but I persuaded them to let me handle it. I told them that you were the man to put Bryant in his place . . ."

Arthur was silent for a moment or two. "This is a ticklish one, Jacob. Bryant is free to discuss controversial issues if he wants . . . Yes, I suppose a lot depends on how he goes about it.

Thanks for ringing me. I'll think about it and see what I can do. Whatever you do, don't *write* anything."

Arthur spent a sleepless night. He tossed and turned. Was Bryant worth protecting? Would he *ever* develop some "nous"? Did he really know enough about Bryant? Shouldn't his deputy have kept him informed of what was going on? Could he really throw his daughter's evidence at Bryant?

Was Bryant in the right? Was he letting himself be prejudiced by relatively minor issues, like the untidy room?

Sleep presented no solution.

EIGHT

DECISION MAKING IN AUSTRALIAN EDUCATIONAL SYSTEMS: CRITICS AND CONCEPTS

Adapted from a paper read at the third Seminar on Administrative Studies in the Research School of Social Sciences, Australian National University, Canberra, August 1965.

INTRODUCTION

For the great majority of people in our society, formal organizations represent a major part of the environment. Schools and other consciously "educational" institutions are formal organizations which influence, either directly or indirectly, the lives of nearly all members of Australian society. Yet, as March and Simon[1] point out, at the present time we know very little about formal organizations of any type, much less formal educational organizations.

The administration of educational organizations has long been dependent for its insight upon folklore, revelations, and authoritative opinions. Clearly, the scientific study of such organizations has important implications for educational administration. Theory, leading to research, may provide us with new insights into the cultural milieu of organizations and into the organizations themselves. There are few aspects of the organization and administration of schools and school systems which do not cry out for theoretical constructs upon which hypotheses might be based and investigation carried out.

In recent years, Australian educators have become increasingly aware of the criticisms levelled at their schools by visiting observers. Much emotionally-toned discussion usually follows the publication of these criticisms, but few, if any, efforts are made to place the discussion into relevant conceptual frameworks, to define terms or to construct and test hypotheses which bear upon the criticisms made.

This lack of attention to scientific analysis is by no means limited to those observed, however. Similar criticisms may be levelled at the reports presented by many observers themselves. For example, most of the criticisms made by visitors centre on a lack of grass-roots decision making in Australian education, the assumption being that such decision making is a valuable component in the apparently more flexible systems best known to the observers. Underlying the grass-roots concept is the belief that the great mass of the voting populace identify closely with the public schools, and through elected representatives directly influence their policies. However, in the United States, for example, political scientists and sociologists have demonstrated rather convincingly that the assumption of grass-roots control of public education is itself a myth. Since the publication of Floyd Hunter's *Community Power Structure: A Study of Decision-Making*[2] in 1953, the term "power structure" has become almost a household word and has provided the impetus for a number of systematic empirical studies. Of these studies Pellegrin comments,

> These investigations have called attention dramatically to one of the outstanding facts about public participation in civic affairs in our democracy—namely, that only a small proportion of the population is actively and directly involved in decision making processes. This is true no matter what area of community affairs we examine—economic, governmental, educational or any other. I know of no study which has found more than three per cent of the adult population actively and directly involved in the decision making processes of the community.[3]

This example is quoted merely to illustrate that the application of social science concepts to education may well produce some unexpected data and challenge some established myths and legends.

The present paper is concerned with a small number of theoretical frameworks to which Australian educators might turn should they wish to take the discussion of the comments made by observers, no matter how distinguished, beyond the limits of opinion and conjecture. More specifically, since most criticisms appear to be levelled at the distance from the man in the street or from the teacher at the "cutting edge" in his classroom, that major policy decisions affecting Australian public schools are made, this paper will be chiefly concerned with presenting theories which, while valuable in themselves, might illuminate one another through the common link of administrative decision making.

ORGANIZATION THEORY AND ADMINISTRATION

At heart we Australians are confirmed serendipidists. We are not at all impressed with the word "theory", which we tend to equate with the word "impractical". Yet, if educational administration is to progress beyond the stage of alchemy, there is no alternative open to us other than theorizing, hypothesizing, and researching.

In previous papers I have concentrated on theory *per se*. However, the chief emphasis here is on organization theory, especially as it has implications for the study of educational organizations and for the behaviour of those who play administrative roles within them. The lines between organization theory and administrative theory are not well-defined. It will be convenient to describe organization theory as being concerned with the dynamics of social systems and administrative theory as being concerned with the management of those systems.

In a theory-oriented paper read to the first Australian Seminar on Administrative Studies in August 1963, Willett[4] pointed out that, ten years previously, a paper such as his would have discussed organization rather than organization theory and its content would have been concerned almost wholly with specific problems of industrial organization. It is pertinent to look at the place of organization theory in educational administration from a similar viewpoint.

The 1964 Yearbook of the National Society for the Study of Education[5] provides an admirable parallel to Willett's experience. Unlike the 1946[6] Yearbook, the last to be concerned directly with educational administration, the 1964 volume places great emphasis upon competence to assess and analyse problems of administration rather than "how-to-do-it" information on how administrators have handled these problems in the past. The writing reflects an acute awareness of contributions to be made to the study of administrative behaviour by the social sciences, and the emphasis is upon producing operational concepts, testing propositions, and developing theories.

If there is one clear opinion which emerges from contemporary thought in university departments of educational administration, it is that no one theory will suffice to guide the researcher. There is an equally clear recognition that theorizing and researching in the area is no small problem. As Schwab,[7] University of Chicago philosopher and geneticist puts it:

> In brief, as an object of research, a school as an administered entity is an animal, a stochastic series of an especially complicated kind. Each given moment of its tenure is in large part the consequence of previous moments of that tenure; each given moment may be filled by a vast number of alternative actions or inactions, each of which will modify in a different way the character of the next moment. If, for simplicity's sake, we freeze the flight of time's arrow, we are still faced with the same high order of complexity that faces the physiologist who attempts to study the complex interaction of parts which constitute a living organism in a relatively steady state.[8]

Schwab points out that the dynamical equations of physics involve three to five terms, of which one or two are constants. In Biology, such items as the Wright and Fisher equations deal with great difficulty and doubt with seven to nine factors. In the social sciences the most complex economic models involve some 50 to 200 terms, many of them only mildly inter-correlated with others. But school administration is shown to involve somewhere between 4,000 and 50,000 terms, almost all of them displaying a high degree of correlation. Schwab shows that the distance between 200 terms and 4,000 terms presents enormous problems, for the needed storage facilities of a computer increase as the *square* of the number of factors involved. Schwab reminds us that the social sciences—the source of the general propositions relevant to educational administration—cannot as yet furnish certain answers, but this is scarcely an argument for their abandonment. The immensity of the problem does not mean that we should cease theorizing. Willower,[9] for example, sees educational science as analogous to political science so far as the uses of theory are concerned. Political science is concerned with the study of a given institutional area. It utilizes the methods of other fields, notably sociology and history, and political scientists do not fear to range wide in the development and application of ideas.

DECISION MAKING AND ADMINISTRATION

Gregg,[10] of Wisconsin, while accepting with Schwab the desirability of a grasp of several theories, seeks to find a meeting point for such theories. In a critique of the 1964 Yearbook referred to previously, he points out that although useful concepts such as decision making, leadership, and organizational equilibrium are explained, they are treated in relative isolation from one another. He asserts that the relationships among the concepts are not at all clearly delineated and there appear to be no common ultimate criteria to which the concepts may be related and tested. Like Griffiths, the editor of the Yearbook, Gregg believes that a common ultimate criterion may be found in decision making, which is regarded as the essence of administration—the basis upon which all other administrative functions can be related and interpreted.

The present paper is intended to go no further than identifying ways in which a beginning might be made in this direction. Decision theory has produced voluminous literature in recent decades. In *Functions of the Executive*,[11] published in 1938, Barnard described decision making as "the essential process of adaptation in organizations". Writing in 1957 Simon[12] asserted in his *Administrative Behavior* that the task of "deciding" pervaded the entire administrative organization quite as much as the task of "doing". Griffiths,[13] writing specifically in the field of educational administration, pointed out that directing and controlling the decision making process was the central function of administration. More recently Dill[14] urged the need for basic research on decision making in educational organizations.

Of particular relevance to Australian researchers is the place of decision making in bureaucracies, since the vast majority of Australian educators work in bureaucratic environments, whether these be governmental, clerical, or in the private sector. In this regard the theories of Presthus[15] (referred to later in this paper) and Argyris[16] may be of particular interest.

A good example of a "decision" theory which appears to have relevance to complex decision making in large bureaucracies is the recent presentation of Meeker, Shure, and Rogers[17] of System Development Corporation. These authors, seeking a suitable typology for characterizing decision situations, regard decision-making man not, like so many economic theorists, as a rational animal, but as a *limitedly* rational animal. Man does not optimize in reaching decisions, he merely suffices, i.e. he chooses the alternative which meets or exceeds all of his criteria, the one that is "good enough". Such a man is faced with two types of choices—rule-following situations and decision situations proper. With regard to decision situations, some, where an available alternative clearly and uniquely leads to the satisfaction of the accepted goal, are *simple* decision situations. But where there is no alternative clearly and uniquely better than the others, a state of indecision or conflict arises which must be resolved. These states are *unacceptability*, when the best of the perceived alternatives will not achieve the desired results; *uncertainty*, when the likelihood of achievement of the desired results by means of contemplated alternatives is unknown; and *incompatibility*, when available but mutually exclusive alternatives are equally satisfactory with respect to given goals.

In their analysis the authors use formulations of procedure —the requirements, standard practices, directives—to which the administrator is committed in actual practice. The initial phase of the analysis should expose all the non-programmed decision areas. For example, *alternatives* are implied in the statement "whenever the situation warrants." *Prerequisites* will be identified: "There are conditions which must be met before a given alternative can be employed." By reference to these prerequisite conditions the subset of alternatives available in a given situation may be specified. Associated with each alternative course of action are sets of *consequences*. Some of these will be efficacious in achieving organization goals; other subsets will be generally prohibitive; but not all will be invariably and constantly efficacious or prohibitive under any circumstances.

One use of this model is its obvious power in delimiting the locus and concentration of decisions in a hierarchy and highlighting the conditions under which decisions are made. The value of such analysis is that it limits itself to specified procedures and does not attempt to convert even simply resolved decision situations into rule–following unless this is sanctioned by formally standardized practice. In view of the often-expressed belief that the Australian Departments of Education are administered in the impersonal, rule-book, inflexible manner implied in the traditional Weberian theory of bureaucratic decision making, this theory may well provide some perceptive insights through the testing of hypotheses on aspects of "Departmental" decision making.

All of the above theories, then, provide hypotheses which might be employed to test assumptions about decision making in Australian educational organizations. However, these examples by no means exhaust the theory sources available, and in this paper an attempt is made to suggest a small number of theoretical frameworks which appear to have value for testing a number of more specific assumptions about decision making at various levels in Australian State Education Departments. Through the use of these theories it should be possible, for example, to ascertain where decisions are made, why they are made, and what effect they have upon personnel at all levels within the hierarchy of the state departments.

CENTRALIZATION AND ORGANIZATION THEORY

Judging from the comments of observers from overseas, one of the major organizational problems facing Australian school systems is the high degree of centralization of decision making which is exercised by the bureaucracies situated in each of the state capitals.

Kandel[18] wrote in 1938:

> A central authority tends to grow by the power which it wields and when such an authority exercises at once, the rights to legislate ... by Orders-in-Council, to execute, and to judge, the result is inevitably rule by a bureaucracy which imposes its will and ultimately secures uniformity in aspects of the educational process where uniformity is least desirable.

Seventeen years later Butts[19] wrote:

> Not only do I find a presumption in favour of uniform policies as good in themselves, but also I find the belief that uniform policies can be maintained on a state-wide basis only by centralizing decision-making in the hands of a relatively few persons.

As recently as 1961 Jackson[20] commented:

> In the two largest states, there are clear indications that retention of the present system of inflexible central control, with little or no real delegation of responsibility and authority, will inevitably bring the whole administrative machinery grinding to a full stop.

These are, of course, quite general statements. Let us now take a number of more specific observations upon decision making. As has been pointed out above, one assumption that is commonly made by observers is that our highly centralized systems are somehow antithetical to the concept of democracy, chiefly because of the lack of local machinery, which in some countries provides opportunities for the citizenry to maintain close contact with and control over the public schools. Related criticisms have been made by Australian authors. One writer asserts:

> The outstanding need of Australian education (is) ... that every citizen should be made to feel that the State school belongs to him, that it is rendering him a real service, that he has obligations in regard to it.[21]

To what extent are these assumptions valid? Are the policies adopted in Australian public schools for example, contrary to the wishes of the majority of citizens? How do societal expectations influence organizational decision making?

The theory propounded by Talcott Parsons[22] may provide an adequate basis for research. Parsons suggests that formal organizations have three levels or systems—the technical, the managerial, and the institutional systems. Clearly, in an educational organization the technical functions are performed by teachers, the managerial by principals, the institutional by the state department, *but also by a superior agency into which organizations must articulate—society itself.* As Parsons puts it:

> A formal organization . . . is a mechanism by which goals somehow important to the society, or to various subsystems of it, are implemented and to some degree defined.

No organization (for example, a school) is completely independent. Its functions and purposes, its resources, its treatment of its students are all subject to higher level controls. Parsons sees three types of control: the generalized norms characteristic of society as a whole, the formal structure which links the managerial and institutional levels, and the political arrangements which bring the organization into direct relationship with the larger society.

The testing of hypotheses based upon this theory might permit us to map, probably for the first time in Australia, just where decisions are made, by whom, and as a result of what social forces.

SYSTEMS THEORY

Turning from societal influences to the internal operation of the organization itself, it is clear from the three quotations above that the observers see the administration of Australian education as epitomizing the classical Weberian concept of bureaucratic control. Writers have often criticized our alleged lack of flexibility in thinking and our apparent lack of interest in innovation. Such criticisms have been so common as to justify a close investigation of the dynamics of decision making by individuals in these organizations.

The implications of the comments made by Jackson,[23] a Canadian, are clear:

> Of course, in a highly centralized system ... in which all teachers are civil servants, only the voluntary agencies on the periphery of the educational scene ... could provide an independent evaluation and criticism of the existing system.

Butts comments:[24]

> The assumptions of a centralized system that a uniform policy must be achieved and that the basic decisions should be made by a relatively few persons in head office reflect this lack of confidence in teachers ...

Criticisms are made not only of the speed of change, but of the direction of change. Butts assumes that in Australian school systems change occurs from the top down, in direct contrast to the alleged "grass-roots" changes of his homeland.

Systems theory provides us with a promising model to investigate the direction of change in organizations.[25] A system is a complex of elements in mutual interaction. An *open* system is related to and exchanges matter with its environment. All systems except the smallest have sub-systems and all but the largest have supra-systems, which are their environments. System theory deals only with *open* systems, which have certain characteristics that distinguish them from closed systems. They

1. exchange energy and information with their environment, i.e. they have *inputs* and *outputs*;
2. tend to maintain themselves in *steady states*, i.e. by a constant ratio being maintained among the components of the system;
3. are *self-regulating*;
4. display *equifinality*, i.e. identical results can be obtained from different initial conditions;
5. maintain their steady states in part through the *dynamic interplay of sub-systems operating as functional processes*, i.e. various parts of the system function without persistent conflicts which defy resolution;
6. maintain their steady states in part through *feedback*, i.e. the feeding back of outputs to the input to affect succeeding outputs;

7. display *progressive segregation*, i.e. the system divides into a hierarchical order of relatively independent subordinate systems.

From this theory, which is concerned with conflict, motivation, and decision making, we can describe, explain, and predict a wide range of human behaviour within organizations. A number of hypotheses concerning change have been derived by Griffiths from this model. Some of these with obvious implications for a centralized system are:

1. the major impetus for change is from the outside;
2. change is more probable if the successor to the chief administrator is from outside the organization rather than from inside;
3. when change in an organization does occur, it tends to occur from the top down, not from the bottom up;
4. the number of innovations expected is inversely proportional to the tenure of the chief administrator;
5. the more hierarchical the structure of an organization, the less the possibility of change.

THE ORGANIZATIONAL SOCIETY THEORY

While systems theory provides an interesting model for testing hypotheses relating to administrative structure, the theory constructed by Robert Presthus[26] seems even more likely to provide useful insights into the behaviour of individual officers at all levels of the hierarchy.

Presthus assumes three distinct levels in modern life: society as a whole, big organizations, and individuals. Organizations he views as miniature societies in which traditional social controls over the individual appear in sharp focus. Accepting Sullivan's[27] interpersonal theory of psychiatry, which argues that most behaviour is the result of the individual's search for relief from anxiety—the tension induced by conforming to authority—and Weber's[28] concept of a bureaucracy as the most efficient form of organization devised by human beings, Presthus claims that big organization induces anxieties in its members simply because of its fundamental characteristics. "The main function of hierarchy", he writes, "is to *assign* and validate authority along a descending scale throughout the organization".[29] The hierarchy is of vital importance, since the individual's participation in an organization is always affected by his place in the hierarchy. The larger the organization, the lower morale drops as individuals tend to feel unimportant. The presence at the head of bureaucracies of oligarchies with a preponderance of power accentuates the anxieties of other members.

Individuals accommodate to the demands of the organization in three ways—upward mobility, indifference, and ambivalence. The *upward mobile* is the most successful organization member. He feels friendly towards his superiors; he accepts the organization's values as decisive; he makes decisions in terms of the organization rather than the individual. The *indifferent* refuses to seek the organization's favours. He develops his major interests *outside* of the organization. His anxieties are reduced to a minimum: "He sells his time for a certain number of hours and jealously guards the rest." The *ambivalent*, the small minority, can neither resist the appeals of power and success nor play the role required to gain them. He places individual friendships above the good of the organization. As Griffiths so pungently puts it, "His is, indeed, a miserable lot in the modern large organization".[30]

To observers of decision making by Australian educational administrators at all levels and to those familiar with the arguments on school administration often presented by teachers' organizations, this theory is of more than ordinary interest.

PERSONALITY THEORY

Some of the quotations produced above imply that teachers and administrators who grow up within a system adopt particular stereotyped "departmental" administrative styles. If this is so it might be predicted that the "system" dominates the personalities of individual educators. Such a viewpoint is reflected in Hemming's claim that

> Many parents, teachers and inspectors still cling to the exploded fallacy that all children of the same age ought to be at the same standard.[31]

With exasperation he adds, "No one expects all boys of 12 to wear the same size suits."

Bush,[32] of Stanford University, obviously implies the existence of organizational stereotypes, at least so far as teachers are concerned.

> The role of the teacher in Australian secondary schools appears to be well defined. The manner in which the teacher is to go about this main function (of teaching) is quite definitely spelled out: a syllabus to be followed; a textbook to be used; a notebook to be kept; a daily pattern of verbal teacher questioning and pupil response to material that has been assigned for home study. While the teacher tends to accept this generally understood version of his role ... he complains of an impersonal but omnipotent force called THE DEPARTMENT that tends to keep him from the full exercise of his creative uniqueness.

Is decision making by teachers or, indeed, administrators, primarily a function of institutional or personality variables? While Getzels'[33] paradigm might provide a valuable model for research in this field, Hemphill's[34] conceptual framework may be suggestive of needed research. Hemphill and others hypothesized a relationship between patterns of administrative performance and person variables only. Thus the style of administration of a principal may be understood in part as an expression of measurable personality characteristics.

Because of the diverse orientations of the research staff who were drawn from a number of academic disciplines and who had various orientations towards the place of theory in research, an overall conceptual framework was developed, no attempt being made in this study to force all views into an integrated or consistent single point of view. There were, however, two identifiable major theoretical viewpoints, one regarding administration as problem solving and the other regarding administration as decision making.

Eight administrative styles were identified:

1. *High communication style.* Principals characterized by this style of work stressed communicating with others about the problems they encountered in their work.

2. *High discussion style.* Principals characterized by this style placed unusually high emphasis upon the use of face-to-face discussion in administration.

3. *High compliance style.* This style characterized principals who generally followed suggestions made by others.

4. *High analysis style.* Principals who were high with respect to this style spent relatively more effort than others in analysing the situation surrounding each administrative problem.

5. *High relationships style.* This style refers to a high concern with maintaining organizational relationships, especially relationships with superiors.

6. *High work-organization style.* This refers to the principal's emphasis upon scheduling and organizing his own work.

7. *High outside-orientation style.* Principals high on this style of administrative performance displayed greater readiness than others to respond to pressures from outside the school.

8. *High work-direction style.* Principals who followed this style tended to stress giving directions to others as an important part of their work.

Might it be possible to test the personality-variable-administrative performance theory in Australian schools through the replication of Hemphill's work? Does the Australian educational bureaucracy in fact prevent the growth of individual "styles" of administration?

ORGANIZATIONAL CLIMATE

Another approach to the question of stereotypes might be made through an examination of some of the assumptions about conformity, uniformity, and authoritarianism in the climate of individual classrooms. For example, Hemming[35] complains that the majority of Australian state schools are rigid and autocratic in social pattern and describes the administrative system as "so aloof and authoritarian that the teachers themselves get no sense of participation in top-level policy making." Kandel[36] writes of uniformity and a certain monotony rather than variety or flexibility as characteristics of the system; of maintaining standards of efficiency which place a premium on conformity. Again, "Originality and initiative are discouraged, and the teacher or headmaster who introduces some experiment or innovation may even be written off by an inspector for 'showmanship'." Butts[37] dolefully quotes from a state syllabus: "The central administration formulates and assesses educational policies and the teacher presents these policies as school organization, lesson materials and teaching procedures in the classroom."

Is it true as is implied, that the centralized systems produce a particular kind of classroom climate? To what extent is classroom climate associated with decision making above the level of the classroom teacher?

Halpin and Croft[38] were struck by the common statement among school men: "You don't have to be in a school very long before you *feel* the atmosphere of the place." This "atmosphere" they refer to as *organizational climate*. Their task was to map the domain, to identify and describe its dimensions, and to measure them. The researchers not only assumed the existence of a "personality" in a school, but assumed that this personality was best studied, like human personality, not by phenotypic bases of pertinence, but by a genotypic approach.

Halpin began by merely *describing* organizational climates, but he soon found that the *quality* of different climates became too vivid and too compelling to be ignored. He hypothesized that numerous factors could be considered as defining the climate of the school—such factors as the socio-economic status of the school's patrons, the attitude of parents, the teacher's salary schedule, the "quality" of the students, and many others. However, to limit the scope of the enquiry the climate was mapped in terms of teacher-principal relationships.

Halpin and Croft identified six climates, from "open" at one end of a continuum to "closed" at the other. They found that a school possessing an open climate was a lively organization, moving towards its goals and at the same time providing satisfaction to the members of the organization. The closed climate, on the other hand, marked a situation in which the group members obtained little satisfaction in respect to either task achievement or social needs. The principal was ineffective in direction, and unconcerned with personal welfare.

"Climate" was measured on eight dimensions, four pertaining to teacher behaviour, four to principal behaviour. The four *teacher* behaviour dimensions were:

1. Disengagement (the teacher is "not with it", the group is not "in gear");
2. Hindrance (the principal hinders rather than facilitates);
3. Esprit (morale: teachers' social needs are satisfied, they enjoy a sense of accomplishment);
4. Intimacy (friendly social relations with other teachers; not primarily associated with task accomplishment);

The four *principal* behaviour dimensions were:

5. Aloofness (behaviour which is formal and impersonal);
6. Production emphasis (close supervision of staff, highly directive);
7. Thrust (effort to "move the organization" through personal example);
8. Consideration (the "human" element).

Is there such a phenomenon as an "Australian" (or a "Queensland" or a "Victorian") classroom climate? How are the observed climates influenced by principals, inspectors, and administrators higher in the hierarchy?

CONCLUSION

In view of the growing importance of formal educational organizations to our society, ventures in education telesis are bound to continue. The observations made by the increasing number of scholars and practitioners visiting our schools should provide interesting fields for investigation. At the present time we do not have an over-riding theory of administration, much less of educational administration. We do, however, have a number of important and promising theories which employ the concepts of psychology, sociology, economics, political science, and other disciplines. The sociological concept of role, or the psychological concept of personality needs, for example, are valuable tools in our attempts to understand organizations, their purposes, and their settings. Another valuable concept is that of decision making, and this is the tool I have attempted to employ to link together the theories presented in this paper.

The application of some of these theories by researchers in Australian education might introduce a measure of scientism into an area where trial and error, whether reported by overseas observers or native Australians, still appears to be the order of the day.

NINE

ORGANIZING THE SCHOOL FOR INDIVIDUAL DIFFERENCES: THE INNOVATIVE ROLE OF THE NON-GOVERNMENT SCHOOL

Adapted from papers read at a conference of the Queensland Assistant Masters' Association, Brisbane Grammar School, Queensland, May 1967, and a conference of school principals, University of New England, Armidale, New South Wales, June 1967.

This paper is concerned with change and innovation. It may seem strange that I should choose to read such a paper to you, for of all the institutions in our society schools are among the most conservative and are indeed often accused of resistance to change.

The Saber-tooth Curriculum,[1] that gentle satire on educational conservatism, remains as much required reading for the schoolman of today as it was for the schoolman when first published thirty years ago. The vivid picture I have of New-Fist turning over in his burial cairn at the thought of the Saber-tooth Curriculum being replaced by another, even though saber-tooth tigers had ceased to inhabit the earth in favour of little woolly horses, haunts me to this day. If the Saber-tooth Curriculum remained one of the eternal verities during the onset of the second ice age, what are the eternal verities of the thermonuclear age? How much of the rationale for what we do when we *teach* today is lost in antiquity?

This paper is being read in a school which, like several other prestigious institutions in Australia, stands for a number of eternal verities which it is patently unnecessary for me to describe. Look around well, for many of our most cherished assumptions, beliefs, hypotheses (prejudices, if you like) about schools and schooling are likely to be challenged in the next decade or so as they have never been challenged before. I say this advisedly and without histrionics for we are on the threshold of quite remarkable discoveries about teaching and learning as, for the first time in history, the social scientist turns the cool objectivity of science upon the myth-ridden, legend-laden practice of teaching.

My paper, I repeat, is about innovation. It will attempt to describe the great leap forward in our ability to research the teaching–learning relationship; it will describe several organizational devices that have developed in response to these researches; it will attempt to describe how leadership becomes innovative behaviour; and it will leave to *you* the question of deciding whether you wish to adopt the role of innovator, and if so, the strategy that you, your school, your department, or your masters' association might adopt.

It may appear that in my preoccupation with teaching and learning *per se* I have by-passed examining. The implications for examining, however, should be clear at every stage of my talk. If not, they should be discussed in a later paper, for as devices for retarding innovation they are the Australian teachers' great alibi.

It is a truism that we live in an age of extraordinary change. When the fine old school in which we meet today was founded, life in the Moreton Bay district was in many ways very little different from life in mediaeval Europe. Man's only form of land transportation was the horse; his lighting was provided by a tallow candle or at best sperm oil; his ice was brought, packed in sawdust, from the great frozen lakes of North America, half a world away; his medical services were little better than those offered by the eleventh century hospital at Salerno; his schools varied little from the rigid, formalized, grammar-centred institutions of the time of Henry VIII.

Consider the changes which a century has wrought: the supersonic jet aircraft is almost a reality; electric lighting has been developed to the stage where Sydney's huge Royal Agricultural Showground may be lit by a single, intensely powerful bulb suspended high over the main arena; refrigeration is employed for a wide variety of purposes ranging from air conditioning to ice-needle brain surgery; medical science has mastered most of the traditional plagues of mankind; and the schools —ah, what shall we say of the schools . . . ?

These examples of change are the most obvious results of the revolutions which have taken place in the fields of technology and the physical and biological sciences. Change in the schools is much less obvious, much less overt. There has, of course, been change, as any student of the inputs and outputs of systems might demonstrate. However it is the *extent* of the change which is being questioned. Of all the formal organizations in our society—hospitals, factories, or retail stores, for example—the schools have remained probably the most conservative, most resistant to change.

Why is this so? Has the Darwinian cue passed them by? Not quite, for it is clear that science has been gradually nibbling away at the assumptions of our educational past. The researches associated with the child-study movement, for example, have had obvious influences on our teaching methods, especially in primary schools. Yet, compared with other professions, the quantity of valid, empirically obtained data with regard to the practice of our profession remains pitifully small.

That this should be so is not, of course, surprising. The behavioural sciences—those that have to do with the behaviour of man, individually or socially—are still poorly developed. While economics has a reasonably lengthy and respectable history, the other sciences—those like anthropology, sociology, social psychology, and political science—have much more recently achieved mature status and academic recognition. But the revolution in the social sciences is at hand. At last there are some of us, at least, who have come to the realization that man, like any other object of nature, can be studied scientifically and, within certain limits, controlled scientifically.

Teaching is partly an art. It is also partly a science. It is clearly a process which should derive its theories and its practical insights largely from the social sciences. Its practitioners, therefore, should rely upon the social sciences in much the same way as medical practitioners rely upon the biological sciences.

Only in recent years have social scientists taken a marked interest in the teaching–learning process. The detailed conclusions of workers like Cornell, Withall, Grimes, Sears, and Flanders need not concern us here, though for those who do not know the monumental volume *Handbook of Research on Teaching*,[2] I refer especially to the name of Nate Gage, now Director of the Center for the Study of Teaching at Stanford University. This volume, perhaps one of the most important publications of all time so far as teaching is concerned, contains contributions by most of the leading researchers in the field. The purpose of the book is to improve the conceptual and methodological equipment used in research on teaching by bringing those interested in such research into more fruitful contact with the social sciences. The conceptual framework of the volume specifies three major classes of variables:

a) *Central variables*, which refer to the behaviour or characteristics of teachers, including teaching methods, instruments and media of teaching, and the teacher's personality;

b) *Relevant variables*, which refer to antecedents, consequents, or concurrents of the central variables, especially social interaction in the classroom and the social background of teaching.

c) *Site variables*, which refer to the situation in which the other variables are studied, particularly grade level and subject matter.

It is not the task of this paper to report directly on research on teaching, however. Our task is to examine some of the implications of such research for the organization of the school and to look for ways in which the non-government school might provide leadership in adopting and developing such organizational procedures. What is the outcome of all this recent research and discussion concerning teaching and learning?

Teaching behaviour has been looked at from many angles. Some have viewed it from the standpoints of emotion, feeling, or ingratiation. Others have viewed it from the standpoint of involvement of pupils. Some have looked at teaching as a system of questions, answers, and discussion. Some, including workers at the University of Queensland, have considered teaching behaviour from the standpoint of the acts by which ideas and concepts are taught. Certainly the emphasis is now upon *observing* teacher behaviour, either directly or with the assistance of such hardware as tape recorders and video-tape machines.

Learning in the classroom is now seen as being largely the result of the teachers' behaviour in initiating and guiding student activities, in reinforcing student responses, and in accentuating student involvement in the learning process.

B. O. Smith of the University of Illinois, and one of the foremost writers in the field, is optimistic about the outcomes of such research. At a recent conference he pointed out:

> At last we have come to grips with our phenomenon; namely, teaching behaviour, and have begun to deal with it on its own terms. We now understand our problems and are beginning to define them in ways that promise practical dividends as they are solved. We are developing techniques of observation and analysis that uncover more basic variables than our earlier naive concepts could reveal. We are taking our research into the classroom and the school setting without losing the precision that our practical solutions require. As our knowledge of teaching behaviour accumulates, the day will come when no child will fail to learn in keeping with his capacity if his socio-economic existence is at an adequate level. This hoped-for day is, I believe, closer than we think.[3]

All of this work on teaching and learning has been going on at a time when interest in the individual abilities and needs of children has attracted great attention. The conclusions reached by workers in both fields highlight the fact that the teaching and learning process is complex indeed; that its bases vary greatly from individual to individual. Thus, some individuals learn best under pressure, others at a more leisurely pace; some learn best in large groups, some in small groups, some individually. There is no simple model to serve all teachers and all students at all times. This realization has led researchers to urge upon administrators the need for providing opportunities for a great variety of learning situations and particularly situations in which children are challenged to work to their own full capacity.

One thing we *have* learnt from the social sciences—or at least from hypotheses derived from those sciences and tested in school situations—is that many of our traditional assumptions about how children learn and how teachers teach are quite unfounded. Consider, for example, some of the implications of recent research—some of them admittedly based on inadequate data and others based on so-called action research rather than the tightly controlled empirical studies which most of us would prefer. Serious questions have been raised concerning our traditional beliefs about pupils' emotional security and personal needs, the optimum teacher-pupil relationship, the size and composition of schools and classes, pupil grouping of various types, school architecture, and the capacities of individual students to work at advanced levels.

Much of the work that has been done in these fields has arisen from the application of the scientific method to some of the pious pronouncements about individual differences and the "uniqueness" of each child which, expressed as "oughts" rather than "is's" and defined in ephemeral goals rather than "operational" terms has plagued educational literature for generations. While educators have long been aware of the implications of individual differences for teaching (and have, on the whole, *ignored* those implications, especially as far as the curriculum, class assignment, and examinations are concerned) some few attempts have been made around the world to devise teaching plans to cater for the differing abilities, backgrounds, and interests of children. The Dalton Plan, the Platoon School, the Winnetka Plan, and so on all have made some minimal impacts on teaching, but none has proved sufficiently influential to affect the teaching procedures of the majority of teachers. One attempted solution, however, "grading according to ability" or "homogeneous" grouping has spread widely in popularity both in primary and secondary schools.

Recent research has shown how extraordinarily great are the differences among and within individuals *and*, crucially, the great variety of ways not at all in keeping with traditional theories of learning and teaching in which pupils in fact *do* learn. Further, this research has shown rather convincingly that the various organizational devices for catering for individual differences, including the much-favoured homogeneous grouping, have had little success.

If it is possible to generalize, then, from the work of the behavioural scientists who have concerned themselves with teaching and learning during the last few years, it is to state that the process of teaching and learning is very much an interaction situation between the individual teacher and the individual child; that in this situation teaching might be effective, and learning effective in situations previously regarded as indefensible or even unworkable; that the greater the variety of teaching–learning situations provided, the greater the possibility of learning taking place.

It is recognition of these facts which has led to the recent urgent upsurge of interest in ways of organizing the school for individual differences. This interest in teaching and learning, coupled with interest in the implications for teaching of individual differences (cf. the National Society for the Study of Education Yearbook, *Individualizing Instruction*,[4] and Bassett's *Each One Is Different*[5]) has coincided with a vastly increased enrolment in secondary schools with consequent serious shortages in teacher supply and school building provision.

Concern with individual differences has not always been expressed as strongly as it might in Australia. In this country, while most school systems would reject the notion that all twelve-year-old boys should wear the same sized suit, most have not got around to accepting the notion that all twelve-year-old boys do not need the same methods of teaching, the same curriculum, the same syllabus, the same academic standards.

In other countries, however, administrators have been bombarded with requests, even demands, for greater variety in teaching techniques, more individual attention to children, more teachers and more teaching space. In a field like educational administration which might almost be defined in terms of scarce resources, not all of these demands *could* be met, but a number of interesting and promising compromises have been reached, particularly in the United States where the combination of the pressures referred to above is at its greatest.

We might discuss some of these innovations briefly, indicating the arguments for and against, and leave it to you to decide whether the idea is worthwhile pursuing. I shall devote a brief space to each of the following:

1. Team teaching
2. Non-grading
3. Flexible scheduling
4. Library-centred school

TEAM TEACHING

The origins of the recent development of team teaching are not clear, though it is clear to me that the system has accepted a number of practices which have been common in universities —those much-maligned centres of teaching—for centuries. Certainly, the work of the Trump Commission headed by Professor J. Lloyd Trump gave a great impetus to interest in the movement. This commission was concerned not only with teaching and learning *per se* but with curriculum development, teaching methods, space arrangements, and staff utilization. The Report of the Commission[6] is a paperback which deserves to be read by every teacher and certainly every headmaster, for it forecasts many of the changes which are taking place— and which I suspect, will take place in many more secondary schools soon. Beginning with the premise that students need to develop the inquiring mind through improved study skills and *individual responsibility*, the commission recommended the more effective use of professionally trained teachers, the employment of para-professional teachers' aides, the large scale revision of curricula and the erection of more flexible school buildings capable of taking advantage of recent developments in technology.

Children were to spend their time chiefly in three learning situations: large group instruction (150 students or more) for 40 per cent of their time; small group instruction (15 students or less) for 20 per cent of their time; and independent study for

40 per cent of their time. Teachers, assisted by teaching aides, were to work together in teams, planning courses, teaching large groups (thus freeing other members of the team for small group work or individual consultation) leading seminars jointly, evaluating progress, and so on. Schools, of course, would need considerable reorganization, especially with regard to library space and facilities for private study.

There are obviously several alternative ways of providing for team teaching or at least co-operative teaching of one kind or another. Robert H. Anderson[7] has set out the requirements for an *ideal* conception of team teaching which need to apply if the full benefits of team organization are to be realized. These are, according to Anderson:

1. All team members participate in formulating broad policies;
2. All team members participate at least weekly in formulating the more immediate objectives of the programme;
3. All team members comment specifically on one another's programme;
4. It should be possible for a man to step into a colleague's teaching shoes in an emergency;
5. All team members from time to time (perhaps every day) teach in the actual presence of colleagues;
6. All team members participate in evaluation including times when *episodes* in his teaching are carefully and objectively analyzed.

Evaluation of team teaching is in its infancy. Most research studies have relied on questionnaires, testimonial evidence from teachers, pupils, and parents, and a few have made use of standardized tests to assess the effects of the organization upon academic achievement. The evidence is, on the whole, favourable towards team teaching, though this is to be expected when the approach is experimental and most of the teachers involved are themselves volunteers.

One interesting—and to some observers, disappointing—aspect of the achievement of pupils taught by this method is that almost without exception achievement as measured by standardized tests has been found to be almost the same as in control classrooms which are self-contained. However, such tests measure short-term outcomes of schools and do not normally concern themselves with the more long-term outcomes, such as growth of enthusiasm for education, efficient utilization of time, skill in locating and analyzing information, and capacity for self direction, all of which may, in the long run (as most university lecturers who are in contact with recent high school graduates soon realize), be of much more importance than the achievement scores themselves.

It is important to realize that team teaching is not in itself a methodology or a system of instruction. Rather it is a stimulant to the analysis of instruction and the development of techniques, yet its importance is clear with regard to pupils, teachers, and headmasters. For pupils, it provides that variety of teaching–learning situations—large group, small group, independent study—with a variety of teachers which current research suggests is conducive to the type of interaction which encourages effective teaching and learning. From the teacher's point of view, its most unfamiliar and probably most difficult to accept aspect is its emphasis upon relentless, continuing day-by-day evaluation. Intimate and continuous exchange of ideas, information, and criticism is obviously an important aspect of the plan. From the point of view of the headmaster, it allows for unusually rich varieties in locating pupil groups of various sizes. It produces some interesting timetabling situations. It makes possible the relatively economical use and effective control of supplies, resources, aids, and buildings. It obviously has built in "supervisory" potentialities, if by "supervision" we mean influencing the professional performance of teachers through such methods as discussion, observation, reading, and self-evaluation.

Team teaching, then, in one or other of its forms is likely to be introduced into Australian schools at an increasingly rapid rate in the future. Of course, like all innovations it will force us —the practitioners at the "cutting edge"—no less than the headmasters, the school boards, architects, and the manufacturers of school equipment to stop thinking of classes of forty children, classrooms like square boxes, and teachers' aides as a joke. Teachers' associations, too, will need to alter their thinking about many cherished prejudices—for example, that against teachers' aides. Teachers will have to think themselves out of their present roles to the new roles which these changes will demand. This, of course, will call for in-service training and strategic supervision by headmasters and other senior teachers.

NON-GRADING

Another important development which stems from much the same philosophical base as does team teaching is non-grading. This system has, in fact, "arrived" in New South Wales primary schools, where there are now rather more than a hundred such schools.

The essential arguments that have influenced the supporters of non-grading have been:

1. There is a great diversity within and between individuals with regard to achievement and potential;
2. The rigidity and inflexibility of schools as we now know them prevents the development of each individual to his full potential;
3. A more flexible organization of the school could help close the gap between aspiration and reality in this regard.

We are all familiar with the arguments against the lock-step type grading of schools and most of us would, I imagine, subscribe to the three arguments cited. Why, then, are we so hesitant to do something about this question? It should not be difficult to "ungrade" a school, "unfreeze" pupils, and record and report pupil progress. One difficulty, of course, lies in the *curriculum*, and this is a major problem in a country where university-dominated external examinations effectively control what is taught in secondary schools.

Under a non-graded system for at least some hours every day each child is working at his own rate—normally in a classroom in which other children of approximately equal capacity in a particular subject also are working. The element of competition in the student's work is not against other pupils, but against himself.

There are several excellent examples of non-graded secondary schools, probably the best known examples being Evanston

Township High School in Illinois and the Melbourne, Florida, High School near Cape Kennedy, which has an outstanding individualized programme–even to the extent of providing students at the senior level with individual lockable studies. The implications of such teaching are likely to provide traumatic situations for Australian teachers used to using books entitled "Fifth Form Mathematics" or "Third Form Algebra"— and let's be frank—it is also likely to produce traumatic situations for Australian book writers and publishers! This trauma does not worry me in the least. The deliberate introduction of some trauma might not be a bad thing for Australian education. The real difficulties, naturally, come in the upper and lower forms of the school. What does Mr. Jones, Maths teacher in first form, teach the obnoxious children from Mulligan's Tank Primary School, a non-graded institution, who have already mastered first form Algebra? And what does Mr. Smith, teacher of Fifth Form English, do with a child whose capacity and interest is obviously of first year university level? Does he force the boy to fit in with his peers, to mark time?

Of course, this problem is not unique to schools. Universities, too, will have to face up to the reality of non-graded high schools sooner or later. So far as I know no Australian university is prepared to enrol brilliant students, who have run ahead of their peers at high school, direct into certain second year subjects, as is done at Harvard.

There is not, as yet, a body of significant research on the non-graded school. The evidence available seems to suggest that children at the extremes of the ability continuum profit most academically, that teachers become more aware of the needs of individual pupils, and that parents' interest in children's schooling seems to grow.

Is there a future for non-grading in Australian secondary schools? I think there is. The developments in the primary schools, the increasing availability of individual work plans like the S.R.A. reading laboratories, and the growing popularity of programmed learning devices, together with a new awareness of the dynamics of the teaching-learning situation, are all

[133]

moving in the direction of non-grading, in spite of the requirements of the external examinations.

As all those who have had experience in timetable construction know, a major problem in providing a range of experiences
and choice of subjects is the restriction placed on flexibility by
the timetable. This is known in America as the schedule. The
scheduling function takes on horrific overtones when the
principal and his staff attempt to introduce that variety in
teaching and learning situations which we have seen is now
considered desirable for optimum learning. The larger the
student body and the more restricted the staff available and the
school plant provided, the greater is the problem of providing
this variety.

The School of Education at Stanford University became
interested in this aspect of school organization when it was
realized that many proposals for innovations made by members
of its staff were impossible to introduce because of the restric-
tions of the timetable. In typical American fashion an approach
was made to the Ford Foundation, and the computer-
based S.S.S.S. or Stanford School Scheduling System is the
result.

The present "egg-crate" type scheduling, based on perhaps
thirty students in a room for fifty or sixty minute periods was
replaced with a basic module of five or more students and fifteen
or more minutes. Almost any teaching configuration requested
could be scheduled quickly and cheaply by the University's
computer service.

When I visited the centre at Stanford last year the following
example of the use of flexible scheduling was provided:[8]

> A tenth grade (fourth form) English course has an enrol-
> ment of 347 students. Time allocated for this course is fifteen
> modules per week, which is comparable to the traditional
> provision (i.e. 15×20 minutes $= 300$ minutes; 5×60
> minutes $= 300$ minutes). A team of three teachers is teaching
> this course. At this point, however, our English course
> becomes quite atypical. Three teachers, as a team, designed

the course that they are teaching; this is a major and important departure.

How did the team elect to use the twenty minute time modules? They concluded that a part of their instruction could be provided for 347 students in one group as effectively as for thirty, with a considerable conservation of time and energy. Further, adequate facilities (auditorium) for large group instruction were available. After due consideration of the material to be presented, a large group meeting (347 students) was designed for two modules (forty minutes) once each week.

The team wanted to provide a weekly classroom opportunity for their students to write. Moreover, they wished to make optimal use of the part-time para-professional aide assigned to their team. For this phase of instruction, a design that would allow a reasonable number of students to write, be tested, or clarify material, was needed. The group size selected was sixty students, which allowed the use of double rooms (sixty-five seats). Further, this situation could be handled easily by one teacher, or proctored by an aide. The time required was a more difficult decision; how long does it take to write well? How long should a test be? Many factors were important in this choice. With considerable deliberation, the writing laboratory was set at four modules (eighty minutes) once each week.

In the opinion of the team, the heart of the instructional process for this course would be the opportunity for each student to ask questions, answer questions of their classmates, discuss new concepts, present material from their own study, and receive personal teacher guidance toward the goals of the course. From the limited experimental evidence available, it would seem that these kinds of activities could best be served in a small group (ten to fifteen students). Moreover, the team wanted a period of time that would adequately provide for thorough discussion, interaction, and closure. Intuitively, they felt that the small groups should meet for at least one hour (three modules). Dictated by the importance of the small group function, they requested two meetings each week for this phase, a total of six modules (two hours).

In addition to these three phases of our English course (i.e. large group writing lab, small group), there remain three modules of independent study (sixty minutes). This time is not scheduled. This is an important factor in the development of the educational potential of a student to allow for the exercise of his own volition in pursuing his academic responsibilities. Our observations to date lead us to speculate that this may prove to be, at least for many students, the most important phase of the learning process.

After the careful professional deliberations of three experienced English teachers, a design for instruction has been formed. What, specifically, has been provided for each student and each teacher? Each individual will be exposed to new information by three teachers. The teachers make best use of their individual competencies; they would have, therefore, three weeks to prepare for each major presentation. Once each week, every student would have the opportunity to write for more than an hour, under supervision, where he will receive immediate feedback and assistance as needed. The two hours of small group meeting will provide close, personal interaction between both teacher and student and the student and other students.

Our example is not the only way, certainly, to teach tenth-grade English. It is, however, in the opinion of the three most important people involved—the teachers who designed the structure—the way in which they can teach most effectively. More important, variations in the structure of English courses permit a new functional level of self-evaluation of the course structure. From this evaluation, new and more appropriate patterns for teaching will emerge.

The three teachers say that they are working harder but on a higher professional plane and with more satisfaction. There is also some additional anxiety, understandably, due to adjusting to a new method of teaching. But more important is their strong personal commitment to "their program" and, consequently, a higher motivational drive toward the teaching task.

Recently I was able to visit five or six high schools which had adopted flexible scheduling. Perhaps the most interesting—and initially, disconcerting—observation was that many students, especially senior students, were not scheduled for any classes at all for approximately one third of their time. In these schools there were always some students sitting in the sun and wandering along corridors, but the libraries and instructional resource centres were crowded and busy to an extent I have never observed in Australia. The schools all reported that disciplinary problems relating to classroom behaviour had declined drastically since the adoption of flexible scheduling. This appears to support an assumption which is gaining ground in many western countries that high school students are capable of assuming a great deal more academic and social responsibility than we have given them credit for.

LIBRARY-CENTRED SCHOOL

From the beginnings of recorded scholarly history, the library has been an important adjunct to, if not the very core of, institutions of higher learning. It was reported that when the Arabs of the Caliphate sacked Alexandria the books from the ancient Greek University's Library provided fuel to heat the city's baths for six months. The provision of a scriptorium in the monasteries of the Benedictines played no small part in that rebirth of learning we now call the Renaissance.

When schools were no more than formal grammar-learning institutions they had little need for libraries, since a few textbooks to be learnt by heart were usually all a student required. Today, however, most of us would regard the library as the real core of the enterprise. Already most of us have learnt to direct our pupils away from the narrow confines of the text to the wider resources of the library. This tendency is likely to increase greatly in the future, especially if such procedures as team teaching, non-grading, and flexible scheduling are introduced. Indeed, their success is largely dependent upon the ready availability of books and other instructional resources including audio-visual devices which can be operated by the student himself. In several schools I visited recently in the United States there were two or even three "instructional resource" centres combining books, magazines, newspapers, audio tapes, video tapes, slide projectors and slides, and even movie projectors equipped with small personal screens and ear phones. The librarian was assisted by aides who, when requested, guided the students' use of resources and by technicians who cared for and set up the electronic equipment.

It is not my intention to say more than this: that the acceptance of *any* of the major theories of teaching and learning or of school organization proposed here implies the availability of library and audio-visual resources far in advance of anything I have seen in Australian schools to date.

LEADERSHIP

Having looked at some of the major developments that are taking place in school organization in an attempt to improve teaching and learning by individual children let us turn to the question with which we began—what has all this to do with leadership?

Let us be clear on what we mean by "leadership". To me a successful leadership act is one which achieves what it sets out to do, i.e. the decision to act is judged successful or otherwise in terms of the outcome of the action which follows the decision.

Clearly it is possible to exercise leadership acts which gain little or no following. While these acts may well display various educationally desirable characteristics, such as the "creativity" and "audacity" much favoured by Theodore Brameld in his *Education as Power*,[9] they are not effective leadership acts in the long run unless that creativity and audacity produces some degree of followership.

It seems clear that the independent school, because of its comparative freedom from bureaucratic controls, appears to be in a position more favourable than most Government schools to display leadership. We might also assume that while the independent school's first responsibility is to serve the children in its care, a second major responsibility *should* be to provide leadership in school organization for the most effective teaching and learning.

If we accept this second assumption then it is important that the non-government school find ways of displaying leadership which are most likely to influence the behaviour of those responsible for the schools. In effect, schools which set out to lead, to innovate, or to change must have a *strategy of action*.

A CLASSIFICATION SCHEMA OF PROCESSES RELATED TO AND NECESSARY FOR CHANGE IN EDUCATION

	RESEARCH	DEVELOPMENT		DIFFUSION		ADOPTION		
	RESEARCH	INVENTION	DESIGN	DIS-SEMINATION	DEMON-STRATION	TRIAL	INSTALLA-TION	INSTITUTION-ALIZATION
OBJECTIVE	To advance knowledge	To formulate a new solution to an operating problem or to a class of operating problems, i.e., *to innovate*	To order and to systematize the components of the invented solution; to construct an innovation package for institutional use, i.e., *to engineer*	To create widespread awareness of the invention among practitioners, i.e., *to inform*	To afford an opportunity to examine and assess operating qualities of the invention, i.e., *to build conviction*	To build familiarity with the invention and provide a basis for assessing the quality, value, fit, and utility of the invention in a particular institution, i.e., *to test*	To fit the characteristics of the invention to the characteristics of the adopting institution, i.e., *to operationalize*	To assimilate the invention as an integral and accepted component of the system, i.e., *to establish*
CRITERIA	Validity (internal and external)	Face validity (appropriateness) Estimated viability Impact (relative contribution)	Institutional feasibility Generalizability Performance	Intelligibility Fidelity Pervasiveness Impact (extent to which it affects key targets)	Credibility Convenience Evidential assessment	Adaptability Feasibility Action	Effectiveness Efficiency	Continuity Valuation Support
RELATION TO CHANGE	Provides basis for invention	Produces the invention	Engineers and packages the invention	Informs about the invention	Builds conviction about the invention	Tries out the invention in the context of a particular situation	Operationalizes the invention for use in a specific institution	Establishes the invention as a part of an ongoing program; converts it to "non-innovation"

In recent years a number of social scientists have become interested in strategies of change and innovation. Some of you will be familiar, for example, with the work of Miles[10] at Teachers' College, Columbia, others with that of Carlson[11] of the Center for the Advanced Study of Educational Administration at the University of Oregon. A valuable schema for our discussion this afternoon, however, is that presented by Clark and Guba[12] at a recent United States seminar on innovation (see p. 139). Guba, incidentally, has recently been appointed Director of the National Center for the Study of Change at the University of Indiana. The schema or model attempts to classify the processes related to and necessary for change in education. Four processes are hypothesized: research, development, diffusion, and adoption. The *objective* of each of these processes is described, as is their *relation* to change.

The first process is, of course, *research* which provides the basis for invention by presenting *ideas*.

The second process is *development* which is subdivided into *invention* and *design*. The objective of invention is to *innovate*, to formulate a new solution to an operating problem or to a class of operating problems. It is this stage which produces the *invention*. The objective of design is to *engineer;* to order and to systematize the components of the invented solution; to construct an innovation package for institutional use.

Thus far we have been concerned with those who research, engineer, and package. An analogy in medicine is the invention of the Salk vaccine and in the engineering which produced it in large quantities at an economic price. The research stage is the concern of the "egg-head", the development stage of both the "egg-head" and the engineer.

The next process primarily concerns the "leg" men—those concerned with spreading the word—the agricultural extension officer in rural industry, the advertising agency in business, the drug companies' medical representative in the vaccine analogy referred to above, the demonstration schools attached to the teachers' colleges in the case of education. This is the process of *diffusion*, of which the first stage, dissemination, seeks to *inform*, to create widespread awareness of the invention among practitioners. The second stage, demonstration, seeks to *build conviction*, to afford an opportunity to examine and assess operating qualities of the invention.

The next process, that of *adoption*, involves the practitioner himself, since it is now necessary to put the innovation to the test of practice. The first stage of adoption is trial, in which the practitioner *tests* the invention in particular contexts, in order to provide a basis for assessing its quality, value, suitability, and utility. The second stage is that of installation, in which the practitioner *operationalizes* the invention by fitting it to the characteristics of the institution in which he works. The third stage is that of institutionalization, that in which the invention ceases to be an innovation; when it is established and assimilated as an integral and accepted component of the system.

Examples of the third process, adoption, are everywhere to be seen: the medical practitioner has tried and adopted the Salk Vaccine; the Queenslanders years ago tried and adopted the cactoblastis insect to defeat prickly pear; teachers everywhere—for good or evil—have tried and adopted the Herbartian steps.

Now, it is important to note that this schema is an "is" rather than an "ought" schema. Although it clearly has implications for those who wish to innovate, it also has value as a means of describing how innovations have taken place and are taking place today.

The study of innovations is a fascinating exercise. Why, for example, has one motor company, the British Motor Corporation, achieved some success with its new big car, the Morris 1800, when its previous big car, the Austin Freeway, was comparatively unsuccessful? How is one to account for the adoption of, say, the Cuisenaire method of teaching elementary arithmetic in Victoria, or of an adapted version of the Illinois programme of secondary methematics in New South Wales, while other programmes have been rejected or, more often, ignored?

It is a sobering thought that at one time in our history the formal institutions we now call "school" were themselves innovations. By what stages did the school change into a "non-innovation"? At the present time we are watching an interesting innovation in the field of politics—the gradual adoption of substantial state and federal aid for independent schools. This innovation remains largely an innovation: it still is in the process of adoption, and then only in certain areas. Why is this innovation moving so slowly? At what stage in the schema is the blockage taking place? Is it perhaps at the stage of demonstration in the *diffusion* process? Have its proponents *built conviction* about the invention?

To return to the central theme: assuming that the non-government school is, in fact, an environment in which innovations might flourish, might it not be that its main function in the schema is to *demonstrate*, to *build conviction* after a period of adoption?

The adoption of such a role, whether the interest be in team teaching, non-grading, or flexible scheduling is, I believe, a proper and necessary function of the non-government school. Success in such a role, however, will depend not only upon the strategy of innovation itself but upon two elements of educational leadership which are demonstrably lacking in Australia today: creativity and, perhaps more important, audacity.

Is it too much to ask for this creativity and audacity from you, the members of an organization which has demonstrated its interest in innovation by arranging and attending this conference? As James Bryant Conant once put it: "Behold the turtle—he makes progress only when he sticks his neck out."

THE FLY CATCHERS: THE ROLE OF A TEACHERS' ASSOCIATION IN THE FUTURE OF AUSTRALIAN EDUCATION

Adapted from a paper read at the Seventy-fourth Annual Conference of the Queensland Teachers' Union, Brisbane, May 1964, and reprinted by permission of the editor from *Queensland Teachers' Journal*, LXIX, No. 5 (1964), 150-61.

The title of this address, as some of you will have guessed, is prompted by Robert Bridges' poem of the same name. Perhaps you remember it:

> Ye recall me a time sixty summers ago
> When a young chubby chap, I sat just so
> With others on a school form, ranked in a row,
> While an authoritative old wise-acre
> Stood over us and from a dish fed us with flies,
> Dead flies—such as litter the library south window,
> That buzzed at the panes until they were stiff-baked on the
> sill,
> Or are rolled up asleep in the blind at sunrise,
> Or wafered flat in a shrunken folio.
> A dry biped, he was nurtured likewise
> On skins and skeletons, stale from top to toe,
> With all manner of rubbish and all manner of lies.

This none-too-flattering recollection of Bridges' school-days serves to remind us not only that teachers have fared badly in our literature, but that teaching has but one prime end—the education of the individual being.

I want to lay great stress on this latter assumption at the beginning of this address because I feel that the lack of public recognition of the teacher as a professional person (with all that this implies in terms of salary, status, and working conditions) which appears to be the concern of every teachers' union in Australia today is inexorably linked with the public's understanding of what goes on between the *individual* teacher and the *individual* child. While those of us who are closely connected with teaching often speak in a blasé manner of the teacher's task as being the transmission of the cultural heritage, those not directly associated with teaching refer to it in much more specific terms—in terms of its effect on individual children personally known to them. In this regard the public assesses teachers in much the same way as it assesses architects, doctors, lawyers, and dentists. The immediate implication of this is that any attempt by a teachers' union to develop a favourable "public image" of the teaching service can succeed only if in the long run the vast majority of individual teachers are regarded by society as being worthy of such an "image".

Before proceeding further, it would do no harm to ask ourselves whether we are justified in asking that the status of teachers in our society *should* be as high as that of other widely recognized professional groups. Is the task of the teachers as important to the preservation and enrichment of society as are the tasks of lawyers, doctors, engineers, and dentists? I want to clear up this point once and for all, for if the answer is "no", my argument and, incidentally, that of the teachers' unions, will not hold water.

There are few fields of human endeavour more plagued by shibboleths and sham than education, and I realize that platitudinous remarks about the importance of the teacher have been common for many centuries. I have tried very hard to be objective in my assessment, and I hope I, in my turn, will not be considered platitudinous when I say that, after deep consideration, I have concluded that there is no vocation worthy of higher status than that of teacher.

Secondly, we are entitled to ask whether, in fact, society does regard teachers as being lower in status than members of the recognized professions. I know of no study—and there have been a great many—which has placed teachers in primary and secondary public schools on a par with the recognized professions. Certainly, teachers have little traditional or historical advantage class-wise. Our Graeco-Christian culture has rarely paid court to the schoolmaster, particularly if he taught young children.

Yet, during the last hundred years or so, and especially during the twentieth century, Dr. Johnson's picture of the teacher as "a pure pedantique swiping his livelihood from the posteriors of small boys" has certainly dimmed somewhat. The status of teachers does appear to have improved considerably but by no means to the extent that the importance of their calling would seem to demand. This continuing public disinclination to award high status is sometimes attributed to many variables: comparatively short periods of training; lower entrance qualifications than those required for the established professions; training in institutions less prestigious than universities; a "bird-of-passage" existence; the generally inferior housing occupied by teachers. But all of this is cyclical argument, for it might just as well be argued that these factors are the effect of low status as that they are the cause of it. A possible —and so much more fascinating for the Freudian—contributing factor is that feeling of inferiority and incompetence which people are alleged to experience in the presence of teachers. Do you remember how the adult population of Liberty Hill quaked in the presence of the indomitable Miss Dove?

During the latter part of the nineteenth century, teachers began to resent the community's attitude towards them, as reflected in their salary and in a hundred other ways, and like so many other occupational groups they banded themselves together, hesitantly at first, into associations which, unlike the teachers' organizations of the past, were understandably concerned more with material conditions than with professional matters. Some occupational groups allied themselves with the Labor movement and became industrial unions, determined to take to the arbitration courts matters which for centuries had been decided on the whim of the employing authority.

[145]

I have no doubt that the influence of the teachers' associations on Australian education has been considerable. Unlike many craft unions, they exercised their unionism with considerable restraint. Realizing their responsibility to their immature educands, they avoided using strikes and other sanctions and relied instead on the more "gentlemanly" and in the long run, perhaps more effective method of negotiation. By negotiation they appear to have won considerable material benefits for their members and, incidentally, for the children in their care.

Yet, for all this, the activities of the unions did not win the material advantages and public respect which teachers considered their due. One reason for this was, I suspect, the great emphasis placed on material rewards and on conditions of work rather than upon professional affairs. I am not suggesting for a moment that the great majority of teachers lost interest in individual children: only that the publicity and methods used by the unions gave this impression, since the unions' interests were avowedly material rather than professional.

The point I am trying to make is that an association of professionally oriented individuals *cannot* with impunity abrogate the fundamental responsibilities of its members. Such responsibilities must, indeed, provide the focus of the organization. The only justification for action by a teachers' union is the furtherance of the educative relationship between teacher and child; in the long run, it is the *child* who benefits. If teachers benefit in the process, this is a good thing.

It might well be protested that Australian unions have always taken this point of view. I do not deny that they have *sometimes* taken this point of view, but I am convinced that the arguments used in this direction have had a shallow ring about them. In my humble but obstinate opinion, the public—those who, after all, pay our salaries and grant our status—are not at all convinced that the welfare of individual children is the prime consideration in the policies followed by teachers' unions.

The claims at present being made by teachers' unions all over Australia and the continued comparisons with recognized professional groups which are being made in some quarters have prompted me to list some commonly recognized criteria of a profession for your consideration. These criteria are based partly on those presented by Ward S. Mason of the United States Office of Education, and partly on those presented in the *Yearbook of Education* for 1953. They are:

a) It is a vocation which is practised as a major source of livelihood.

b) It is a terminal occupation.

c) It gives precedence to the occupational role rather than to some other social role.

d) Its members control some esoteric knowledge, not available to the public.

e) It displays a measurable difference between the gifted amateur and the average professional.

f) It leads to clearly demonstrated and substantial social gains from improved techniques, organizations, and philosophy.

g) There is public recognition of special competence in a limited licensing system.

If these criteria are valid they indicate areas which should be of special interest to teachers' unions, as they are concerned with the status and conditions of teachers. I am assuming their validity and I intend to discuss them as indicators of the present situation in the light of what I know about Australian society and Australian Teachers' Associations.

1. *It is a vocation which is practised as a major source of income.*

I do not think we need to spend any time on this one. The great mass of Australian teachers and teachers' unions recognize this only too well, and it appears to be accepted by most members of our society.

2. *It is a terminal occupation.*

This means that people enter the occupation not as a stepping stone to some other occupation, but for the sake of remaining in the chosen field. On this criterion I suspect that Australian male teachers show up very well: they enter teaching with a view to becoming teachers, and once teachers they usually remain teachers. In a recent study I found that at the end of their first year of teaching, no less than 84 per cent of ex-students of the Armidale Teachers' College and the University of New England were committed to a lifetime career in education, 71 per cent of them as classroom teachers. Ninety-five per cent of males expected to be still teaching five years later. This is a very high degree of commitment (assuming that people will do as they say)—probably one of the highest in the world.

The women, however, present a very different picture. Only 8 per cent were committed to education as a lifetime career, 6 per cent of them to classroom teaching. Only 6 per cent of the women expected to be teaching five years later. If these figures are applicable to a wider population, women, who constitute rather more than half of the Australian teaching force, regard teaching not as a terminal occupation, but as a *contingent* occupation. They will teach *if* they do not marry; *until* they have children; *when* the children are of school age, and so on.

3. *It gives precedence to the occupational role rather than some other social role.*

The information presented above suggests that in the case of most women teachers the social role of wife and mother may take precedence over the occupational role of teacher. This is, of course, as it should be, but it must be quite clearly recognized that a predominantly female occupational group is likely to find the achievement of professional status as defined here an extremely difficult task.

I suggest that the movement towards equal pay, so much beloved of some teachers' unions, will exacerbate this difficulty. I wish to make it quite clear that I do not object for one moment to the principle of equal pay for the sexes. All that I am trying to say is that in occupations in which women predominate, the employing authority in the long run begins to think in terms of a base salary which will keep a single woman, or a married woman supplementing her husband's income, in reasonable comfort, rather than one which will keep a married man with a family in reasonable comfort. This is precisely what has happened in the United States where school boards are now busily looking for means of supplementing male salaries.

It is likely that the proportion of women teachers employed in Australian schools will increase in the future, especially as the mores of our society make it easier for married women to return to work. One of the great achievements of Australian education until recent years has been its capacity to hold and attract mature male teachers who, in spite of their grumbles, loved teaching *qua* teaching and brought to the children of the nation a stability of staffing and a continuity of practice which remains the envy of many other educational systems. If the teachers' unions wish to meet this criterion in the future, they will have to find ways of retaining a substantial proportion of male teachers, and I suspect that within three or four decades this will be a much more difficult task than it appears at present.

4. *Its members control some esoteric knowledge, not available to the public.*

Do teachers in fact possess such knowledge? I doubt it. The task of the teacher involves teaching and learning, but little of an esoteric nature is widely recognized, or, indeed, known in these spheres. Research into the strategy of teaching is in its infancy; there is no generally accepted theory of learning. There is, however, a great deal of theorizing going on in these areas and it would be competent for a person who studied solidly in the field of educational psychology and sociology for several years to claim some knowledge of an esoteric nature.

For several years Australian teachers' unions have been urging the necessity of a university degree for all teachers. Rarely has the reason for this demand been made crystal clear. More often than not the move has been supported because it has been realized that the mere possession of a university degree bestows upon its owner a status and salary range hallowed more by tradition than by logic. Often it is argued quite cogently that the teacher thus equipped has a better mastery of his subject matter (some of which, at the higher levels *might* be regarded as esoteric) and hence makes a better teacher. Some brave souls—a small minority, to be sure—have even argued that experience in the university assists teachers to develop that capacity for critical thought which should underlie all education. Rarely has the case been argued on the advantages which might accrue to school pupils *as learners* rather than as examination answerers. Never, in my experience at least, has it been argued that teachers should possess degrees because at the university they would gain some esoteric knowledge, as distinct from subject matter, about the teaching-learning process, which is, after all, the teacher's prime concern.

Herein lies the real stumbling block to the achievement of professional status by teachers. The public is not convinced that there is some esoteric knowledge available to teachers in either *what* they teach or *how* they teach, and who can blame them? The teachers are not convinced themselves. Nor, indeed, are the universities, some of which shy away from the preparation of teachers while showing little hesitation to prepare dentists, veterinarians, business administrators, and traffic engineers.

5. *It displays a measurable difference between the gifted amateur and the average professional.*

In medicine and engineering, for example, there is an impassable gulf between the amateur and the professional, one which cannot be passed by the amateur without grave and immediate peril. In the realm of teaching, however, every parent and nearly every person is at one stage or another an amateur teacher, and sometimes a very successful one at that. Whether or not there is a measurable difference between the gifted amateur and the average professional teacher, we cannot demonstrate at this stage.

6. *It leads to clearly demonstrated and substantial social gains, improved techniques, organizations, and philosophy.*

Generally, most members of the public would agree that teachers do contribute to some extent in this way, though it would probably be argued that university lecturers were more important contributors. Studies of the outputs of education are, as yet, not sufficiently disciplined to help the teachers' case.

7. *There is public recognition of special competence in a limited licensing system.*

The fact that in Australia the licensing of teachers is either non-existent or so nominal as to be almost meaningless is a clear and discouraging indication of the community's attitude towards teaching. And, in the present state of our knowledge, I cannot see any teachers' union convincing the public otherwise.

Our performance on these criteria is discouraging, to say the least. The editors of the 1953 *Yearbook of Education*, in which most of these criteria appeared, concluded that only a small elite of the educational hierarchy can claim to be professionals. They ask: "What of the others? Is the pill too bitter to swallow, to be classed with clerks, draughtsmen, pharmacists, printers, or the hundreds of other honoured and indispensable adjuncts to the learned professions?" They argue that if teachers wish to raise their status substantially, they should inform the lay public of their contribution, engage in collective bargaining, and become a guild of skilled and honoured craftsmen. However, they do not rule out the possibility of the teacher some day coming to command that esoteric knowledge which is clearly the key to professionalism.

I go far beyond the cautious advice of the editors. I believe that there is an esoteric basis—or number of bases—for teaching and learning, and that they are not far from our grasp. I believe that when they are isolated and synthesized they will change materially a great many of the practices which we take for granted today.

I wish to stress, however, that we are going to be able to isolate these only after extensive theorizing and research—only after we have disciplined ourselves to accept the assumption that the whole key to the study of any field of education is an understanding of the teaching-learning process. To do this we shall have to cast away our long-standing pathological eagerness to steer clear of this key process. This avoidance is by no means limited to universities, or to teachers, or to teachers' unions. It is a syndrome of the entire educational fraternity. For centuries, we have avoided coming to grips with the heart of the educative process—and where has it got us? For much longer than sixty summers teachers have been parodied and jeered at, and little boys, in desperation, have whiled away the dreary days by watching the flies on the window pane. We have come to regard ourselves as "practical" men eschewing theory like the plague, because it might be "wrong", forgetting that even "wrong" theory leads to progress.

Our head-in-the-sand attitude has contributed greatly to that poverty of theory and experimentation in education which we take so much for granted. I think I am on safe ground when I assert that I know of no field of human endeavour in which less progress has been made during the last three-quarters of a century than in teaching and learning.

All of this is most discouraging for teachers' unions, for most of their arguments for increasing the status and salary of teachers boil down to the claim of *expertise*. But we have no proof that our expertise is based on knowledge any more esoteric than that of any number of skilled occupations. Hence, not only is it important for the small boy more interested in the fly on the wall than in a fascinating lesson on cube roots, but it is crucially important for teachers who wish to claim professional status that we put aside our fear of theory and our suspicion of research and turn our skills, human resources, and money to where it will matter most.

I am now going to argue that the one great contribution that teachers' unions can make to the future of Australian children and teachers is to help teachers find, identify, and understand those basic processes which are the sole justification of their existence. This will cost money—money for scholarships, fellowships, travel, research grants and visiting speakers. It will also cost goodwill—readiness on the part of the teachers to have their classrooms invaded by "headshrinkers" from the universities, and effort on the part of teachers invited to share in experimental projects. It will cost mutual understanding—a realization that individual teachers, the teachers' unions, and the university faculties of education have agreed to trust one another, to share facilities and to work for the welfare of children.

If I hear mumbles of protest at these suggestions I can understand, but not sympathize. If it is argued that facilities and finance already exist for these activities I can only reply that they are negligible and that they certainly have not been taken advantage of to any extent. If it is argued that such support for theorizing and researching about teaching and learning is not the function of a teachers' union, I can only reply obstinately that in the long run the status of teachers in society is going to be conditioned by what we do or do not know about teaching, and if that is not the business of a teachers' union, what is?

I hope that this address has not given the impression that I am opposed to teachers' industrial associations: I am not. If I were opposed I would not retain my membership in one of them. I do, however, consider that the social milieu of Australia in the remaining years of this century will demand of teachers' unions emphases in policy and practice which are very different from those employed in the rough and tumble of the earlier years of the century. The traditional activities of the unions will continue—for teachers must have a voice in democracies where organized action remains a potent force in converting abstruse statements about the "nobility of teaching" into concrete coin of the realm, and where regulations prevent teachers from publicly commenting on education—but with more finesse, as befits the century of the *Hidden Persuaders*; with more insight; with a more critical attitude towards non-material matters than in the past. In the interests not only of teachers, but of children, the teachers' unions will need to develop a "public image" which reflects the genuine concern of teachers for the well-being and development of each individual child, and which reflects the scientific approach to teaching which I hope will lift the accumulated ignorance of the centuries. There are, I know, ferocious dragons in the path. Let us mount our chargers and confront them, one by one. They are:

1. *The public*

There is no need to remind you that in matters of status and salary it is the public that is the final arbiter. The assertion that "No man is an island" is as true of civil service commissioners,

[153]

arbitration court judges, and politicians as it is of ordinary mortals, and with the best will in the world these decision makers are not going to grant to teachers salaries, conditions, or privileges which their own experiences as members of society and, usually, as fathers of school children, suggest are unrealistic or ludicrous.

I am fairly certain (though I cannot cite research results, for to the best of my knowledge no teachers' union has bothered to find out) the public image of teachers is far from the image teachers see of themselves. On the whole teaching appears to be regarded as a fairly "cushy" job with short hours, long holidays and good pay. It is well known that the job attracts young people who have not attended the "best schools" or who have not managed to be born into the "best families". It is well known, too, that having persuaded young people to enter teaching, we bond them in case they wake up to its frustrations and disappointments too early in life. Teaching lacks the urgency and glamour of other occupations. There are few T.V. teacher heroes. There are so *many* teachers, it is claimed: so many of them young, so many of them women, so many of them doing a really good job of baby sitting. There is no professional body which imposes discipline on its members and which deregisters unsatisfactory teachers. That is all taken care of by the Department, we are told, but nearly every parent I know claims to be able to point to at least one grossly incompetent teacher!

2. *Teachers themselves*

I suspect that the whole question of teacher status is complicated by three factors, all suggested earlier in this paper, which in the future will have to actively exercise the minds of union members. They are the facts that

a) a high proportion of teachers are women
b) a high proportion of teachers are very young
c) a high proportion of teachers originate in the lower social classes.

My own particular stereotype of a teacher is a middle-aged man without a university degree, with two or three children of his own (which are three good reasons why he hasn't got a university degree!) singularly devoted to his job, living in a school residence sadly in need of a coat of paint. I suspect that a great many of those who constitute the real strength of most teachers' unions—the male, young to middle-aged assistant teachers—have a similar stereotype. The preservation of this stereotype suggests that we are living in the past. In those areas in which the public comes into closest contact with teachers as persons, i.e. country towns and city suburbs, the typical teacher is a young, single person or a married woman. Married, middle-aged men teachers appear to be becoming a rare commodity in primary schools. In some schools the only male member of staff is the principal; in others a principal may well have no more than one or two experienced teachers in a staff of eleven or twelve.

I do not intend to say any more about female teachers at the moment (for the wrath of Juno is already upon my head), but I suggest that a very large proportion of teachers will be young, unmarried persons for years to come. And our beginning teachers *are* young. The non-graduates, the vast majority in any Australian system, are actually out teaching, doing the job, at a time when the members of the recognised professions are still less than halfway through their university courses.

The whole picture is complicated by the lower middle–lower class origins of teachers. As Professor Bassett has demonstrated there been no marked change in the social origins of teachers over many years (at least, in the teachers' college in which he carried out his research). Thus, the trained teacher does not typically come from a home where books are cherished, learning is revered, and professional traditions of service and selflessness are accepted. Those of us who have taught in teachers' colleges are only too well aware of the extraordinary—and, I suspect, almost hopeless—task facing a college whose staff is expected in two short years to mould professionals out of youths seventeen years of age whose range of experiences have often been restricted to small towns, whose cultural activities outside of the high school have been almost non-existent, whose lack of social graces is appalling and whose peer group continues to frown on the use of good English as "unmanly".

There was a time, before the advent of the Commonwealth Scholarship Scheme, when teaching attracted some of the very brightest boys from these social classes. Now, with the possibility of more lucrative careers before them, we cannot even count on the lower middle and lower class groups to put their best boys to teaching.

One result of all this is that the young teacher (especially the young male) is quite immature socially, professionally, and scholastically when he takes up his first appointment. He may display initiative, enthusiasm and energy, but in the eyes of the parents and citizens, he remains a rather unpolished, well meaning youth with plenty of money to spend, but so much younger, so much less experienced, so much one of the plebs, with so few professional secrets compared with the young architect or the young dentist down in the main street.

3. *The teachers' union itself*

If I have painted a bleak picture of developments in our vocation, it is because the future looks bleak to me. I am convinced that unless some of the obvious tendencies in teaching are not quickly eradicated, the status of teaching in primary and secondary schools will decline considerably during the next half century. It is my opinion that teachers will have to pull themselves up by the bootstraps, and that teachers' unions can, if they wish, materially assist this process of elevation.

In an age when the public service, like private enterprise, is becoming more interested in the training of administrators, and in the psychology of influence generally, the teachers' unions might well find themselves out-manoeuvred if they do not take steps to meet employing authorities on their own ground. In my experience there is a need for a much more polished, subtle approach on the part of teachers' unions. We need to remember that while one man is beating his head against the stout front door, it is possible that another has unlatched the back door and crept up the stairs. I suggest that nothing but good would result from the attendance by leaders of unions at courses like those offered at the Australian Administrative Staff College, where leadership, management, planning and strategy in operation constitute much of the curriculum.

Let us look again at the questions of teacher recruitment. If I were asked to suggest a policy deliberately designed to deter brilliant and ambitious young men from entering teaching, I would unhesitatingly plump for promotion by seniority. In institutions like schools, where excellence can be the only acceptable criterion, promotion must depend only upon ability and potential—not upon years of service. The rigid acceptance of the principle of seniority, which I am sure survives in many schools, quite clearly demonstrates that schools are regarded not as places which exist to provide the *best* education for children, but as places in which the interests of children take second place to the occupational demands of teachers. Such a viewpoint smacks of professional suicide.

Earlier I referred to the difficulty of making professionals out of young people in two short years. I do not think that there can be any doubt that the real shaping of a teacher takes place once he is appointed to a school staff. I do not want to make this a lecture on school administration, but I feel constrained to point out that there is little hope of teachers seeing themselves as professionals if they do not have the freedom to act as such in their schools. There is overwhelming evidence from experience and research (for, incredibly, the study of school administration is a much more advanced study than the study of school teaching) that teachers who are encouraged to participate freely in school policy making and action taking are more effective, happier, and more professionally oriented persons than those who are not so encouraged. The "nineteenth century" headmaster who expects his teachers to behave like automatons is unlikely to contribute to the professionalism of the individual teacher, for in his view, he *alone* is the professional (L'école, c'est moi). What will the teachers' union do about this living anachronism?

Within the larger sphere of the state teaching service, what will the unions' role be? Will they urge the establishment of Educational Commissions to control state education, or will they favour state boards of education containing representatives not only of the Education Department and the Teachers' Union, but of the parents' organizations as well? Or will they be content to accept their existing relationships with the state? Is it possible that teachers' unions will realize that their members are the "Organization Men", and that they will begin to seriously question the advantages for children and teachers of huge centralized education departments where often, in spite of outstanding leadership, lack of initiative, experimentation, and originality are so obvious? What organization is better qualified than the teachers' organization to adopt the role of the child's advocate, to argue, to reason, to prick the pretensions of bureaucracy?

Finally, will the unions carry out some soul-searching on their own behalf? Will they ask themselves why their members are not at meetings? Why do as many as 90 per cent of members vote on their feet by staying away, as I observed at a meeting in Queensland last year? Are teachers enjoying such prosperity that the unions' policies are no longer a source of strength? Where are the women members?

Soon some of the unions will desire to publish histories of their activities. When they do so let us hope that their introspection will be objective and honest. Let them hand the task to a reputable historian. Let them not gild the lily. While we should be proud of our achievements—where we can show that they are, in fact, *our* achievements—we should not give the impression that unions can do no wrong.

It is obvious that in the interests of both teachers and children the teachers' associations will be just as urgently required in the future as they have been in the past. The associations will need not only to continue their traditional practices of negotiating salaries and working conditions, urging the non-employment of unqualified personnel and the necessity of a university degree for all, but they will need to set out consciously to attract male teachers, to delay the appointment of immature persons, to convince teachers of the importance of their individual contribution to the corporate image, probably through the widespread adoption of a code of ethics.

All of these things they will do because on the surface, at least, they *seem* to be good things to do. However, I cannot stress too strongly that anything approaching the achievement of professional status as defined earlier is quite unlikely until such time as we convince the public that:

a) our prime concern in all matters is the welfare of individual children

b) teaching has an expertise in its own right, growing out of an esoteric knowledge that can be applied only by a skilled practitioner.

The first of these we can impress upon society by our attitudes and actions, both individual and corporate, written and spoken. This involves little more than an attempt to re-educate teachers who may have come to regard a school as a place which provides them with a job rather than as a place in which children learn.

The second of these cannot be convincingly demonstrated without painstaking and disciplined research, which is expensive in terms of both money and talent.

Most of us love our little fly catchers in a way which Robert Bridges and few parents can appreciate. We *know* and we *feel* but as yet we cannot *explain*. Is it too much to ask that you, the most sympathetic towards, the most understanding of, the child's problems, should take the lead in supporting the search for the dynamics of teaching and learning? Without these basic understandings, we can never really become professionals, become truly, as Sir Percy Nunn put it a half century ago: "Ambassadors of society to the kingdom of the child."

ELEVEN

OBSTACLES TO FREEDOM IN OUR SCHOOLS: PUBLIC SERVICE BOARD OR EDUCATION COMMISSION?

Adapted from a paper read to a conference of the New South Wales Branch of the New Education Fellowship, University of Sydney, October 1965, and reprinted with permission of the editor from *New Horizons* XXXV (Autumn 1966), 23-31.
In 1969, three years after this paper was written, the New South Wales government rejected the proposal for an Education Commission.

The theme of this conference is "Obstacles to freedom in our schools". Perhaps I should point out immediately that, not only as a member of the New Education Fellowship but as a student of educational administration and organization in Australia, my own views on the importance of freedom in teaching are substantially in accord with those expressed by the organizers of the conference.

The organizers hypothesize that our schools need to deal imaginatively and creatively with the growth of children and that spontaneity, informality, and free expression are essential ingredients of education. With these hypotheses I have no quarrel. Indeed, as some of you will know, I have myself put this viewpoint in a chapter in Cowan's recent book *Education for Australians*.

Their other major hypothesis—that teachers and principals are restricted by bureaucratic regulation from carrying out a really professional and creative task—is acceptable to me if the word "restricted" is interpreted to mean by indirect rather than direct means, for there are few formal controls which specifically prohibit professional and creative behaviour.

In this paper my argument is based on three key assumptions.

These are:
1. that the main stream function of the school is the cultivation to the maximum of the child's capacities;
2. that the key to this cultivation is found in the intimate teacher-child relationship; and
3. that this relationship is truly educative to the extent to which the teacher feels free (not *is* free, but actually *feels* free) to adapt his teaching to the needs, interests, and abilities of the individual child.

It follows that the proper criterion for judging the excellence of a school system is the extent to which it encourages and supports this adaptability. Therefore, a school system whose administration makes it difficult or impossible for a teacher to develop this adaptability cannot be a good one.

All too often papers on the reform of the administration of education begin with the assertion that such reforms will be in the best interests of the teachers or of the system or of "efficiency". Rarely do the proponents of the reform seem anxious to demonstrate its importance for the individual child in the classroom. This is unfortunate, for the only valid measure of the success of an educational organization or, indeed, of an administrative decision in education, is its effect upon the individual child.

I have discussed the relationships implied above in *Education for Australians*, but I prefer to take my case from another source. Fortunately, in my capacity as editor of the *Journal of Educational Administration*, I recently received an excellent article in this field from Professor F. Enns of the University of Alberta, and I shall take the liberty of quoting at length from a section of his paper. Professor Enns writes:

> Learning is active and individual. It takes place only when the individual is ready and when he is motivated. The individual can be helped to learn, but it is doubtful if he can be "taught" very much. Thus, learning can best take place in an atmosphere of stimulation, freedom from restrictive influences, and in a psychologically supportive climate . . . Good teaching in this sense requires great skill, sensitivity, adaptability and flexibility. It depends upon intimate, subtle

interaction between teacher and learner. It requires all the professional ability and art that a teacher can muster. This kind of teacher behaviour is highly individualistic and can flourish only if and when the overall atmosphere is sufficiently permissive and stimulating.

Professor Enns continues,

> In response to social and economic trends we have tended to develop large, centralized school systems. While the large system has more resources and can use them more effectively and efficiently than the small one, it nevertheless does develop some aspects which tend to reduce the warmly intimate relationships and rapport which are so important in teaching and learning. It therefore becomes one of the functions of administration to counteract the impersonal, demanding, often threatening aspects of the large organization—the bureaucracy—so that the professional person can exercise as much of his professional talent and skill as possible, in spite of the restrictions which may exist. Rather than hold the teacher to the requirements of the system, the administration should attempt to free the teacher from at least the extraneous organizational demands, and to take these demands upon itself. The professional needs to be free to practise his profession.

The question we are discussing today is clearly of more than local or even educational significance. It is of concern to bureaucracies everywhere, be they public or private, and it has long been of interest to students of organization theory. Presthus, a noted sociologist, in his recent book *The Organizational Society*, develops a theory linking Sullivan's interpersonal theory of psychiatry (which argues that most behaviour is the result of the individual's search for relief from anxiety, i.e. the tension induced by conforming to authority) with Weber's concept of bureaucracy. He claims that big organization induces anxieties in its members simply because of its fundamental characteristics. The hierarchy is of vital importance, since the individual's participation in an organization is always affected by his place in the hierarchy. The larger the organization the lower morale drops as the mass of individuals tend increasingly to feel unimportant.

There is evidence to suggest that Presthus' theory would provide a suitable model for the study of our great state educational system. Certainly, evidence from the large number of observers who have commented on our schools is convincingly in consonance in this regard.

I shall not bore you with quotations from the publications of Australian and overseas scholars who have written reports, but no doubt the works of Cramer, Cunningham and Philips, Kandel, Hemming, Butts, Tibble, Bush, and Jackson, for example, are not unknown to you (see Chapter 8). If I were asked to summarize the arguments presented in the sometimes scholarly and usually perceptive reports prepared by these men, I would say that they saw Australian education as marred by mediocrity, conformity, and lack of adaptability in individual teacher/individual child relationships. They were usually struck with the efficiency with which we do things in education, rather than with the *importance* of the things we do. I must say that, in general, and allowing for my rejection of some individual points raised by the above authors, I agree with their assessment. My personal assessment is based on associations (some very close, others rather tenuous) with schools in several Australian states, North America, and Great Britain.

Why is there this apparent lack of adaptability? The answer, according to the authors above, almost invariably lies in the highly centralized nature of our state systems. With this assessment too, I concur, though I would hasten to add that my criticism is not of centralization *per se* (for there are obvious advantages in a measure of centralization), but in *over-centralization*. By centralization I mean the process of leaving most decision making to a central body. For example in England, salary scales are decided by a central body; primary school curricula are decided upon by individual headmasters. In Illinois, decisions on state-wide minimum qualifications for teachers are made centrally; the employment of teachers is a local matter. By *over-centralization* I mean the process of leaving all, or nearly all, major decision making to a central body.

Perhaps when, as in New South Wales, there is not one but three important bodies controlling education—State Parliament, the Education Department and the Public Service Board—we need to look for a new superlative to describe the extent of our centralization!

On the surface, the system of control is delightfully simple. Policy making is the responsibility of State Parliament; execution of policy is the function of the State Education Department; the efficiency of execution is checked partly by other government departments such as the Auditor-General's, but chiefly by an independent body, the Public Service Board. The doctrinaire simplicity of this tripartite division of responsibility into deliberative, executive, and regulative is quite misleading so far as education is concerned, for as we have seen the educative process is far too complex, far too human in its implications to be compared with the operation of a railway system or a postal service.

Students of Australian education have long been aware of this difficulty and over the last decade or so they have noted a tendency to blame the Public Service Board for all the faults of our system. Yet it would be a gross injustice to blame the Public Service Board alone for our teachers' obvious lack of desire to "leap the bonds of earth". There are clearly other formal controls whose effects are deleterious, to say the least.

The restrictive influence of externally set examinations on the secondary schools is widely appreciated, but this can hardly be blamed on the Public Service Board. Nor can the almost childlike acceptance by secondary teachers of university control over syllabuses through matriculation requirements be attributed to the Board. The system of inspection of teachers in New South Wales in its essentials pre-dates the Board by nearly forty years. The distribution of centrally provided curricula is hardly a Public Service Board responsibility.

These evidences of external controls are disturbing to one concerned with the intimate, subtle interaction which should exist between teacher and learner, but even more disturbing are evidences of conformity, lack of innovation, and worship of centralization within the teaching profession itself. In recent

years there have been several examples of the central administration's attempting to loosen its control over areas of the
educational enterprise. By and large the attempts have been
aborted by the teachers themselves. The introduction of the
Wyndham Scheme in the State's secondary schools—providing
unparalleled opportunities for experimentation and innovation
—set up a howl among teachers which has still not died down.
There were constant complaints that teachers wanted to be
told what to teach, what to do, and incredibly, how many
periods were to be devoted to each subject. There were similar
professionally disturbing scenes when teachers urged the re-
introduction of the external intermediate certificate a few years
ago. Recent attempts by the Director of Primary Education
to delegate wider discretionary powers to principals have proved
by no means popular with many principals. Headmasters of
our great high schools for all their security and seniority rarely
set out to test the limits of their discretion.

Just in case representatives of independent schools in the
audience are feeling smug about what I have been saying,
I remind you that so far as I can see the independent schools,
with a few notable exceptions, have done very little in the way
of educational innovation to justify remotely their use of the
term "independent".

All of this is very disturbing, for it seems clear that the
teachers of New South Wales may not yet be ready to accept
the challenge which a proposed Educational Commission will
present. Perhaps my judgment is too severe. There are clearly
some teachers who, in theory at least, deplore this state of
affairs. An editorial in the teachers' journal *Education*, on
10 June 1964, expressed views very similar to those presented
by Professor Enns. The editor wrote:

> In education there is no place for rigidity of control. The
> work of the teacher is such that he must have some freedom
> of thought and expression. If he is denied this, then the educa-
> tion system in which he works will be restricted both in the
> work it does and in the way it develops.

I shall return to this point later on.

Let us now turn to the issue which I have been asked to discuss today: that of the Public Service Board *v.* an Education Commission. The question we must ask is: "Would the replacement of the Public Service Board by an Education Commission contribute to adaptability in pupil-teacher relationships?"

Before continuing with this discussion let us look a little more closely at the Public Service Board.

The Public Service Board was established in terms of the Public Service Act of 1895. Its function was to "abolish all patronage with respect to appointments and promotion in the Public Service" and "establish and ensure the continuance of a proper standard of efficiency and economy in the Public Service". Originally, it consisted of three members whose term of office was limited to three years, but later amendments to the act instituted permanent tenure, i.e. until age 65 (1919), and increased the membership of the Board to four (1955). Members of the Board are removable from office only by a vote of both houses of the legislature and share the immunity of judges of the Supreme Court of New South Wales.

When re-formed in 1902, the Board was responsible for officers in a small number of government departments. At that time there were about 13,000 public servants of whom rather less than 6,000 were employed by the Department of Public Instruction. Fewer than 250,000 children were enrolled in the schools. Today the Board is responsible for more than twice the number of government departments and more than three times the number of employees. Teachers alone now number more than 30,000 and there are more than 750,000 students in schools and technical colleges.

If time permitted, we could look more closely at the Board, noting its judicial and legislative powers and tracing the growth of its functions over more than half a century, but no real purpose would be served by this exercise. Suffice it is to say that the Board, which has numbered some very competent men among its members, has done a great deal with probity, and usually, dignity, to ensure the economy and efficiency of the Public Service. Certainly as an alternative to patronage and confusion, the system has worked well.

What it has *not* done (and in this regard it is difficult to decide between the responsibility of the Board and of the Department) is give the teachers of the state a sense of freedom, a desire to test the limits of their discretion, a genuine encouragement to experiment with and diversify their teaching techniques. It goes without saying that it has certainly not satisfied the salary demands made by teachers.

Throughout the twentieth century tense relationships between the Board and the Department of Education have been obvious from time to time. Peter Board, Director of Education from 1905–22, for example, repeatedly made it very clear that he was exasperated by the Board; and the historic clash between Alexander Mackie of Sydney Teachers' College and the Public Service Board is well documented.

That the Board appears to have done so little to free teachers is most unfortunate, but, perhaps, inevitable, for the Board is not the only agency exercising formal and informal controls over the schools. Perhaps the Education Department itself is more deserving of censure than the Board. Our over-centralization merely gives point to the assertion of Cornell and Inabnit that "the more formal the organization, the more predetermined the lines of interaction are inclined to be, the more relationships are inclined to be guided by the defined role rather than the individual personality".

But all of this discussion has got us only a very little way, for we are still left with a situation where neither the Board, nor indeed the Education Department, has effectively "freed the teachers" to the extent we would desire. Writing a few years ago, R. McKinnon advised Canadian provincial education departments "to untie bureaucratic apron strings, and *trust* rather than run its schools". Perhaps it is time we proffered this advice to our own department and board.

It seems, then, that in the future our chief concern should be with "untieing bureaucratic apron strings", with relaxing controls, with decentralization, if you like.

But what does the future hold? Few promises of relaxation of controls, I am afraid, in spite of the fact that the premier of the state has promised representatives of the Teachers' Federation that he will establish an Education Commission to take over the functions of the Public Service Board. The exact make-up of the Commission proposed by the Premier is not known, but the Teachers' Federation plan has received wide publicity.

Briefly, the Federation's proposal is for the establishment of an Education Commission subject to parliamentary control through a responsible Minister. The Commission is to consist of five members chosen triennially—two elected by the New South Wales Teachers' Federation, two appointed by the Government, and a chairman acceptable to both parties. It is proposed that the Commission will be responsible for the formulation and administration of education policy, including the control of teachers. However, it would not supersede the Director-General of Education, the Director of Technical Education, nor the Technical Education Advisory Council. Unfortunately the exact functions of the Commission are not stated. Nor is it clear whether it will retain the present powers of the Public Service Board or whether some of these will be handed over to the Director of Education.

One's first reaction to this proposal is one of regret, for it represents little more than an attempt to replace one over-centralizing authority by another. It is easy to acknowledge that the Commission has a number of features which will make it more attractive to teachers than is the Public Service Board, but some of the teachers' public statements and implied assumptions on this issue are naive, to say the least.

It will pay us to look briefly at the arguments presented by the Federation in support of its case. It is perhaps pertinent to note—and I shall return to this point later—that the Teachers' Federation claims make no more than passing reference to what the proposed Commission would do to improve the education of *children*. The reasons advanced are heavily teacher oriented, which, at this stage at least, bases their whole argument on criteria rather different from those I applied at the beginning of this paper.

I would not like this statement to be interpreted as implying that most teachers are not interested in the welfare of the pupils in their care. In fact, they are strongly committed in this regard. I do not think it is an exaggeration to say that the parsimonious citizens of New South Wales enjoy a much better educational system and a much more committed teaching service than they deserve. My point is that in spite of its claims to the contrary, the public image of the Federation is not one of a devoted, committed professional association. From time to time the Federation asserts that its prime concern is not the narrow sectional interests of teachers, but the publicity statements too often have a hollow ring about them.

The teachers' arguments are:

1. *The inclusion of Federation representatives on the Education Commission will ensure that the viewpoint of teachers on salaries, working conditions, teacher training, recruitment to the profession, etc. . . . will receive a fair hearing.*

We can agree with this claim on the level of theory, but we would be indeed naive to imagine that the Commission, or any such body, would be in a position constantly to satisfy the demands of teachers for improved salaries and conditions. The recent developments in regard to the Teachers' Tribunal in Victoria should amply demonstrate this argument, if one were needed.

2. *The administration of education by educationists will ensure that policy is made on the basis of educational need, instead of economy.*

Surely this is one of the most naive statements ever made by the Federation. While it is possible that there may be a greater recognition of educational need, it is futile to think that the demands of economy will not loom large in the decision making of the Commissioners. After all, it is most unlikely that the Commissioners will be human islands, free from the pressures of the budget and the national economy, and of competing commissions and boards. If one needed a good example of the way in which an independent commission has drawn closer and closer to a Public Service Board with regard to salaries and conditions of work in recent years, it is necessary only to look at the movement within the Australian Broadcasting Commission towards parity of salary and conditions with the Commonwealth Public Service Board. There is no reason to expect that similar moves would not take place within states. As Howitt points out in Spann's *Public Administration in Australia,* many statutory authorities confer regularly with the New South Wales Public Service Board with the aim of reaching some uniformity of salaries and working conditions with Public Service Act employees.

There is another aspect to this problem—the question of the funds allocated to Education by the Treasury. The Federation may rest assured that the Treasury will be consulted *before* any salary determination is made. Again it may rest assured that the Treasury will not hesitate to draw attention very quickly to any glaring anomalies between rates of pay for teachers and for public servants in other professional and semi-professional positions.

Again, who are the power figures within the Treasury? The decisions of Treasury are largely political ones. The task of identifying the real source of political power has fascinated man from the beginning of recorded history. In recent times efforts have been made in the United States to identify the real decision makers in education, so far with only limited success. To the best of my knowledge no Australian scholar, and certainly no teachers' association, has yet looked at this crucial area of decision making with the same thoroughness and insight which marks Kimbrough's American study *Political Power and Educational Decision Making.*

3. *Because it will be free to devote all its attention to education the Education Commission will be able to undertake long-range planning so that the size of classes can be progressively reduced, the period of teacher training can be lengthened, and the school leaving age raised to sixteen.*

The only section of this sentence which is meaningful, in view of our confusion over responsibilities for decision making, is that which points out that the Commission will be free to devote all of its time to education—an undoubted advantage over present practice.

4. *The setting up of an Education Commission will remove education from the bureaucratic control of the Public Service Board, and restore to parliamentary control through a responsible Minister those aspects of education which at present cannot be decided without reference to the Board.*

First, I think we should be quite clear that although education will be removed from the "bureaucratic" control of the Public Service Board, it will immediately be placed under the "bureaucratic" control of the Commission. One bureaucracy may well be preferable to another, but bureaucracies they both remain. It is difficult to see how the proposed Commission would operate without a fairly large secretariat. After all, the number of officers under its control is likely to be greater than the total number of officers employed by the Public Service Board two or three decades ago. If, as the Federation claims, the Commission is to be concerned with policy making, it will certainly need inspectors or other senior officers to remain in close contact with the Treasury, the Minister, and such departments of government as Education, Public Works, Child Welfare, and Public Health. Presumably it would also need to keep very close links with the Public Service Board, especially if the clerical division of the Education Department is to remain under the control of the Board. As I pointed out above, no-one has stated clearly the responsibilities of the proposed Commission, but I see little likelihood of its not recruiting an extensive secretariat within a few years of its establishment.

Quite apart from the employees of the Education Commission itself, who would certainly constitute a bureaucracy, it behoves the Teachers' Federation to look closely at itself in this light. How large is the Federation? How bureaucratic are its procedures? Frederick Enns saw this point clearly when he wrote,

> and just to keep the record straight, delegating a measure of control to a teacher organization does not in any way reduce the probability of centralization and bureaucratic operation.

In one section of its notes for members, the Teachers' Federation criticizes the Board's legislative power. It points out that under the act the Board has the authority to make regulations which have the force of law, and that although these regulations

[171]

must nominally be approved by parliament, their submission to parliament is a mere formality. Once the regulations have lain on the table in parliament for a specified period they become law unless some member raises an objection. The notes point out that this rarely, if ever, happens, so that the Board has virtually unrestricted authority to make whatever laws it likes affecting the public servants under its control.

The only comment that need be made at this stage is that the Education Commission is likely to have similar powers, and that if there is something wrong with rule by regulation, then it is wrong whether controlled by the Board or a Commission. In fact, I doubt whether we shall ever see the end of rule by regulation, and I suspect that if an Education Commission is established, the regulations it leaves on the table of the house will be very little different from those at present promulgated under the Public Service Act!

5. *The delay involved in referring matters to the Public Service Board will be minimized under the Education Commission, because the Commission will not have to deal with matters referred by other departments.*

This *may* be so, but much will depend upon the efficiency of the Commission's servants. Recent complaints by hospital administrators about the work of the Hospitals Commission may provide an interesting analogy here.

6. *The contribution to education which the Federation will be able to make through its representatives on the Education Commission will enhance the status of the teaching profession and attract more and more highly qualified people into the teaching service.*

The status of the profession may well be enhanced by its representatives on the Commission, but much will depend upon *who* the representatives are! The latter assumption in this statement is very questionable, to say the least.

This argument raises a number of points which I attempted to clarify in an address to the Queensland Teachers' Union in 1964. I argued somewhat as follows: Some teachers' organizations seem to assume that if they try hard enough they will develop a public image of teachers as a body which will win them the professional status and salaries which they consider they so richly deserve. But this assumption is very much open to doubt. By and large teachers receive the kind of salary and conditions the public considers they deserve. It judges teachers exactly as it judges doctors, lawyers, and dentists, i.e. through personal professional contact. Policy makers, arbitrators, judges, are not isolated from the society around them. Law is made and interpreted by such men. The law, with all its implications for the education of children and for the material benefits of teachers, is a living phenomenon. It is made and interpreted by men whose attitudes and opinions are shaped by the society in which they live. It follows that teachers' federations who believe that they will raise the status of their members merely by membership on a commission are just not facing up to the realities of life and law. In his classic book *The Nature of the Judicial Process*, Benjamin Cordozo pointed out in 1921 that law is fashioned by living men, that judge-made law is one of the realities of life:

> The final cause of law is the welfare of society. Logic and history and customs and the accepted standards of right conduct are the forces which singly or in combination shape the progress of law.

The lesson of this is that teacher status is likely to be improved significantly only when society is convinced that the expertise and professional devotion of the *individual* teacher to the *individual* child in his care warrants such status.

7. *The Education Department deals with human material, with children who cannot be treated as mere statistics. An Education Commission would make possible a more human, more flexible approach to problems of children and teachers.*

This is, of course, a definite possibility. This point, relegated to last among the Federation's arguments, is surely the most important of all.

Where does all this discussion of the Teachers' Federation case get us?

[173]

Not very far, I am afraid. I am prepared to concede that the Commission *might* do much for *teachers* in this state, and that consequently the children of the state might benefit. But frankly, I see little in the scheme to assist teaching to become that subtle, innovative, creative activity described by Professor Enns.

The basic question I must ask is why are there *two* authorities in addition to Parliament to control education? Is it not possible to conceive of a single authority to control the public schools? Is it impossible for the Minister to set up a partly elected, partly nominated State Council or Board of Education on which the teachers' organization is substantially represented? If the decentralization of educational administration is quite beyond us (and I fail to see that it is) then we must be prepared to accept cheerfully a measure of bureaucracy in the worst sense of the word. But why two bureaucracies rather than one?

I do not think there can be any doubt that the main reason for the Teachers' Federation's support of an Education Commission is closely tied to an understandable interest in salaries and working conditions. But it should be as easy for teachers to negotiate with a single authority as it is to do so with one of two authorities. If satisfaction were not attained there would no doubt be provision for resource to the arbitration court.

The Victorian Teachers' Tribunal has already demonstrated the lack of wisdom of the "divided control" approach. While there is fairly general agreement among teachers in that state that the "professional" Tribunal is a more satisfactory master than the dominantly "clerical" Board, it would be foolish indeed to claim that all is well in Victoria.

I see no reason why a state board (or commission, if you like) responsible to the Minister and constituted precisely as suggested by the Teachers' Federation, but with the Director-General of Education serving as its chairman, should not have complete oversight of the work of the Education Department. This would leave policy making where it properly belongs—with parliament—and executive and deliberative action where it properly belongs—with the department. It would allow the permanent head of the Education Department to exercise his full deliberative and executive powers with the advice and co-operation of the teachers themselves.

Such a body would throw an even more challenging gauntlet at the feet of the Teachers' Federation. I confess to considerable trepidation in making this proposal, but sooner or later it *has* to be made. Enns poses the dilemma very well:

> Too frequently we take the position that ... professional freedom would be fine if all teachers were adequately prepared professionally and sufficiently committed to accept it. Because they are not, they cannot be trusted to do the right things. This is the old dilemma: which comes first, professional responsibility or professional freedom? I would hold that unless teachers are granted professional freedom, they will never be able to develop full professionalism.

Applying this assertion to the point at issue, I feel that the teachers of this state, at present chronically unprofessional in so much of their behaviour, will become professionals only when they are placed in a position where they can share in policy making which vitally affects themselves and their immature charges. In the *long run* I see important reductions of organization pressures upon teachers and the consequent growth of adaptability in the classroom. In the *short run* I see the obvious advantages to children no less than teachers of working under the authority of one bureaucracy rather than of two.

It would be indeed optimistic to claim that this proposed commission would free the schools to a significant extent, for the number of powerful centralizing forces remaining is far too great—and far too seductive to the mass of teachers who have not learnt to accept responsibility for policy making or even for minor decision making. Yet it promises some relief and it suggests exciting possibilities to the optimist. I for one look forward anxiously to the time when our routinized, stereotyped concepts of what constitutes teaching are replaced by the spirit of Martin Buber's *Teaching and Deed*:

> The influence of the teacher on the pupil, of the right teacher on the right pupil, is not merely compared to, but even set on a par with, divine works which are linked with the human maternal act of giving birth.

[175]

TWELVE

AUSTRALIAN EDUCATION: THE NEXT TEN YEARS

A paper read to the National Conference on Adult Education, University of New England, Armidale, August 1968. Reprinted, by permission, from *New Horizons in Education* (Summer, 1968), pp. 7-16.

Prophecy, though good fun, has always been a fairly "chancy" occupation, even in times infinitely more settled and less complex than the world we know today, so I have reluctantly decided to play only a limited role as prophet in this paper, and to devote as much of my time to talking about what should be done, as to what I expect will, in fact, be done.

The one essential point that must be made from the outset is that education is a *political animal*. This is so in spite of important economic and social overtones, and irrespective of whether it is provided by the state, the church, or some other body. The purpose of education is often defined as the transmission of the cultural heritage, but in fact it is clearly concerned with the transmission of only selected parts of the cultural heritage, and it is in the selection of those parts, in the differing emphases given to them and in the allocation of personnel and capital resources to transmit them, that the political nature of the beast is most obvious.

It is, therefore, a meaningless exercise to discuss the future of Australian education, even in the short run, without taking cognizance of the major social forces which are likely to shape political decision making during the next decade. These forces, not necessarily in order of importance, would seem to include:

1. The further development of Australia's role in South-East Asia, following the gradual British withdrawal from the region.

2. The further strengthening of economic, cultural, and military links with the United States and especially Canada.

3. The further growth of technology and the adoption of automation in not only the so-called secondary, but also in primary and tertiary industries.

4. The further escalation of the knowledge explosion coupled with the cyclical demand for yet more and higher level formal education.

5. The further recognition of the need to plan for the development of national resources, including specifically human resources.

6. The further narrowing of the gap between the so-called urban and rural cultures.

7. The further growth of the ecumenical movement and of concomitant religious toleration.

8. The further growth in numbers and political sophistication of teacher and citizen pressure groups concerned with the improvement of formal education.

9. The further growth in the tendency to look to Canberra rather than to state capitals for leadership in almost all spheres of Australian life.

10. The further growth of the practice of consultative management not only in industry and commerce, but in school systems and in individual educational institutions.

The likely impact of this by no means complete list of social forces upon Australian education in the future is only too obvious. We could devote the whole of this paper to a consideration of the effects of only one of these forces upon a single segment of our education. Instead, we shall concern ourselves with likely developments or at least needed developments during the next decade at each main stage of the educational ladder.

We need to begin by stressing that the most impressive, the most all-pervading fact about Australian education today is the lack of any overall plan to co-ordinate and rationalize the educational enterprise. National enquiries have been conducted into university education and into other forms of tertiary education, but those levels which affect the great mass of Australians and upon which the development of general

[177]

prosperity and citizenship so much depends—the primary and secondary schools—have been largely ignored in Canberra. Politicians in the national capital are still apparently content to strengthen the head and shoulders of the educational animal while permitting the torso—including the very heart of the animal—to stagger along on spindly legs.

As yet there are few signs that Australians are convinced of the importance of investing seriously in human capital. According to UNESCO, the proportion of the Gross National Income spent on education in 1965, for example (4.3 per cent), compares very unfavourably indeed with the percentages spent by Italy (6.5 per cent), United States of America (6.5 per cent), Denmark (7.4 per cent), and Canada (8.5 per cent). Such figures are, of course, notoriously unreliable, but even allowing for a generous underestimation of, say, 1.5 per cent, we have a long way to go to catch up with the Canadian effort. It is true that the amount spent by Australia has increased from 3.06 per cent in 1959-60, but the one per cent increase does not necessarily represent a real improvement in educational expenditures in view of the rapid increase in the population of school age.

Of course, for years educators have felt certain that investment in human capital was the most rewarding investment of all, but they have not succeeded in persuading politicians of that "fact". In very recent years, however, the economists—especially those associated with the Organization for Economic Co-operation and Development—have begun to concern themselves with the inputs and outputs of education—and as we all know, if there is one scholar who quickly gets the ear of the politician it is the economist!

The time is drawing near when the findings of the economists, coupled with other pressures such as those from teacher and parent organizations, will almost certainly force Canberra to take a hard look at education *in toto* instead of at odd parts of the whole which seem interesting from time to time. There is a need for a national enquiry into education at all levels, and there is a need for a central planning body consisting of educators, economists, and sociologists to make recommendations regarding rationalization of resources, accreditation of academic qualifications, interchangability of superannuation schemes, and so on.

But we would be less than honest if we did not recognize that commissions of enquiry and planning groups are usually hamstrung through the lack of adequate and relevant research data. Any Australian bodies set up will certainly not suffer from an embarrassment of riches in this regard. It is to be hoped that substantial Commonwealth funds—at least as much as is set aside for research into wheat growing or military equipment—will be invested in research into Australia's most valuable resource, her human capital.

The questions I am asking here were well put in the United States context in the *Carnegie Quarterly* for Spring 1966. After pointing out some of the things we *do* know about education in the United States, the author continued:

> The only thing we don't know is what is produced by all these teachers, buildings, laboratories, and dollars . . . We cannot describe how close our schools come to accomplishing what they aim to accomplish, identify in any precise way the strengths and weaknesses of the system, or measure progress or lack of it over time . . . The schools are attacked and defended without solid evidence to support the claims of either attackers or defenders, and public policy is perforce made largely on the basis of assumption and impressionistic and incomplete evidence . . .

The same comments could, of course, be applied to Australian education at all levels where we seriously lack "hard" data and rely upon myths and legends about education which have changed little since the days of Plato. Perhaps before long we shall see Australian policy makers looking for data of the type now being sought in the United States by Ralph W. Tyler of the Center for Advanced Study in the Behavioral Sciences in his attempt to find the Gross Educational Product. Certainly, we should be able to look confidently to the Commonwealth to support with more than a mere pittance the research activities of the Australian Council for Educational Research and the University Faculties of Education.

There are good overseas precedents for such financing in the Regional Laboratories and Research and Development Centres supported by the United States Office of Education, in the Schools Council supported by the English Department of Education and Science, and at the state level—and hence even more noteworthy—in the support of the Ontario Institute for Studies in Education by the Province of Ontario.

The importance of such activities for educational planning was put to the October 1967 International Conference on the World Crisis in Education by Mr. René Mahew, Director General of UNESCO:

> If serious, effective work is to be done, at least *two per cent* of the educational budget should, in my opinion, be allocated to research. Hardly anywhere is this percentage reached, although it is well below the corresponding figures for industry and national defence. Paradoxically, our modern societies invest infinitely less money in research concerning the training of the rising generations—not to mention that of adults—than in research concerning steel and cement manufacture, oil extraction or rubber production. Yet the former is a far more complex and mysterious process, with a far more valuable end product—and an activity in which a considerable portion of the budgets of states and individuals is involved. In such an important enterprise we surely cannot indefinitely go on making do with traditional recipes and empirical hit or miss.

Meantime, lacking such data we are forced to rely upon intuition and past experience in our attempt to take a bird's eye view of the next ten years. We shall proceed by levels.

Infant and primary education

Of all rungs on the educational ladder, profound change is least likely to occur at the infants and primary level, for such change is not so necessary. Schools of these levels, charged with the task of providing mastery of certain basic skills, but more importantly of ensuring socialization, have long been more receptive to innovation and change than have more senior institutions. It is clear that Australian society is much less worried by and concerned about these schools than those on higher rungs of the ladder. The reason for this is not, I suspect, lack of parental or citizen interest so much as the conviction that such schools do make a conscious effort to meet the needs of society as a whole, and that the teachers are concerned with children as children rather than as buckets to be filled with knowledge or as examination-dominated machines.

So far as kindergartens and infants' schools are concerned there are few signs of dissatisfaction with the prevailing Froebel-Montessori ethos, though we might reasonably expect innovations in both teaching method and in curriculum in the course of the next few years. We may well see, moreover, some organizational experimentation in the expansion of the non-graded infants' school, at present regarded suspiciously by teachers and administrators reared on the concept of the teacher as a "mother hen".

The chief problems of the sub-primary schools will almost certainly centre on the questions of capital and personnel resources. With regard to pre-school kindergartens, for example, there is already an unsatisfied demand for places, which is sure to be exacerbated by the increasing proportion of mothers who will go out to work. In all states a shortage of not only qualified teachers but of trained teachers' aides will be almost inevitable—unless, of course, society in general and the Federal Government in particular are converted to recognize such schools as having an importance approaching that of Colleges of Advanced Education or universities. And in the absence of research to the contrary, who is to say that in terms of the nation's long term goals they are in fact of less importance?

The primary schools, at least, are widely recognized as an essential step in the educational ladder, if only because they prepare children for the "real" education they are to receive in secondary school. The primary school will, in some ways, be the most fascinating of all educational institutions to watch closely during the next decade. As the very foundation stone of our culture it might be expected to reflect the rather fundamental political changes referred to at the beginning of this paper. How quickly in response to economic and immigration developments will the school's "Australianizing" role grow in importance? How quickly will the history books play down English glories and play up those of the Americans and Japanese? How subtly will the geographers de-emphasize Europe and emphasize Asia and the Pacific? When will Canadian literature and Filipino folk tales filter into the syllabus? Will language teaching in the primary school, an almost inevitable development in the future, concern itself with Asian languages or will it concentrate on good old French or German? Will our military commitment result in a new emphasis on physical education as in the second decade of this century?

The secondary schools, too, will certainly make tentative moves to reflect these new interests, but it is to the much less conservative primary schools that comparative educators might look for the core of a country's thinking. National concerns are etched nowhere more deeply than on the hearts of her primary school teachers.

Turning from curriculum to teaching personnel, a development which will concern all Australians will be the gradual demise of the male primary school teacher. His death is likely to be long drawn out, as in Scotland, but there can be little doubt that within a decade or so there will have occurred a serious erosion in the ranks of the males. What are the implications of this for boys and for society in general? Is the alleged "momism" of the American school something we should consciously emulate? If not, what steps might be taken to counteract it? Is this a proper task for educational planners? Perhaps the question is tied up with the future of the one teacher school, which, in the Australian environment, seems to demand a male teacher. Perhaps the use of educational television (bounced off satellites?) and the use of helicopters rather than buses will render the majority of such schools surplus, though admittedly this is not likely to occur in the course of the next decade.

Organizationally, it seems likely that increasing attention will be paid to variations of non-grading. The fact of the matter is that after two thousand years of Western educational endeavour we are still far from achieving our long-desired goal of individualized instruction. Perhaps a combination of team teaching, non-grading, and programmed instruction will at last permit us to give individual children the attention they need and deserve, but in view of past experience I would not be sufficiently sanguine to suggest that Australian primary schools could achieve that end within a mere ten years or so.

Secondary education

In spite of a notably conservative past it would be very surprising indeed if the secondary schools of Australia returned to their rigid uniformity of the 1930's and 1940's. Every state in the Commonwealth has held its enquiry into secondary education—carried out, of course, in the best Australian tradition by those *within* the system rather than those outside it— and while none of the new schemes adopted is really revolutionary, some (and especially those introduced in New South Wales following the publication of the Wyndham Report) have resulted in important changes. In spite of internal reforms, however, one outstanding (and disturbing) fact remains—the domination of the secondary school by the academic demands of university entrance. For more than half a century groups of teachers and educators generally have attacked this domination, though they have done little to alter it. Today, when teachers are very well represented—and indeed, are often in the majority on curriculum panels—they still, as a group, seem to be prepared to kowtow to the academic standards proposed by university personnel. Fifty years ago Peter Board, that grand old man of Australian education, exclaimed that decisions about what is taught in secondary schools were the prerogative of secondary school teachers. We are still, in fact, far from achieving Board's ideal, though there are signs of change in the air.

The next decade will almost inevitably see the introduction of objective general knowledge papers for the purpose of selecting students for university entrance. It is fascinating to note that after a century or more of criticism of externally set examinations at the end of the secondary school programme coupled with serious questioning of the reliability of many such examinations, it is less educational theory than administrative difficulty which has led to the first tentative steps towards experimental computerized examining of an innovative nature for matriculation purposes, notably by the Australian Council for Educational Research in co-operation with a number of universities.

Matriculation itself is likely to take on a new meaning as it becomes increasingly a requirement for entry to a wide range of tertiary institutions and not only to universities. Some form of matriculation common to all, or at least a group of institutions, is almost certain to develop, possibly on the basis of a points system pioneered in Australia by Macquarie University and now being emulated by other New South Wales universities.

Of course, the common matriculation by itself provides school pupils with no necessary relief from university entrance requirements. Such relief will occur only with the adoption of general knowledge examinations as suggested above or of some form of accreditation. The latter alternative is perhaps more acceptable educationally speaking and it is quite possible that certain Australian universities will emulate their New Zealand counterparts in this regard, but a major problem remains in that we Australians have tied so many scholarship provisions to externally set examinations that they will probably remain, in one form or another, for years to come.

Irrespective of what kind of examination system survives, there seems little doubt that shortages of well qualified staff will enforce the adoption of some form of team teaching, including the appointment (despite the predictable opposition of some teachers' associations) of teachers' aides.

A concomitant likely development is the introduction of modular timetabling which provides time in modules of say 20, 40, 60, 80, etc. minutes for large class instruction, small group seminars, or individual study and consultation. The scheduling of this form of timetabling will probably involve not only excellent library facilities, but the use of a computer, especially to cater for the programmes of large New South Wales high schools. However, this is hardly an insuperable problem.

The problem of adequately teaching greatly increased numbers of students with a relatively small number of well qualified teachers will also suggest the use of programmed instruction and other forms of individual teaching derived from the new technology. Judging from responses to such programmes to date, it might reasonably be predicted that Australian schools will be very slow to take advantage of them. Satisfactory progress in this regard will depend upon our ability to think ourselves out of an educational rut in which one teacher to X number of children is the norm. We shall have to try very hard to convince our colleagues of something doctors have long recognized—that a good machine operated by a competent technician can, in certain respects, do a much more successful job than a busy professional.

Clearly, well designed programmes for use in teaching machines or language laboratories could be of great value in the teaching of information and skills which are likely to be in short supply for years to come—notably in fields like Asian languages and the physical sciences. Their use is obviously desirable, but Australian teachers will need to learn something from experience in the United States, where the preparation of programmes, accompanying books, etc. has become very much the area of big business. If teachers in this country wish to avoid domination by such organizations they will need very soon to begin writing programmes for publication by local university presses or perhaps publishing organizations set up by teachers themselves.

With increasing public interest in secondary education it is likely that the question of optimum high school size will become a matter of debate and, one hopes, of research. The present Australia-wide practice of building high schools to accommodate only a thousand or so pupils seems, on the face of it, downright wasteful, but perhaps a continuation of the work of scholars like Barker and Gump in Kansas, U.S.A., and Campbell in Queensland would help our policy makers in this respect.

There are, of course, many social implications for the secondary school of the future. With the ages of puberty and marriage decreasing steadily it is only a matter of time before married, even pregnant, students will seek enrolment in senior classes. It is only a matter of time, too, before public demand forces the schools to become less coy about sex instruction and preparation for marriage courses generally. The time might even be close at hand when we will be forced to make agonizing choices between such traditional liberal studies as French or Latin and such basic "survival" studies as Driver Education. Nor can we close our eyes to the possibility that before long this isolated Asian pocket of European culture might well, in the interests of its own economic and physical survival, be forced to impose on schools curricula which include compulsory courses in the Australian constitution, in Asian language, in marketing (distributive education, as the Americans call it), and in physical education.

Can we—should we—allow the secondary school to become a deliberate instrument of national expansion or even survival? Will we have any choice in the matter?

Tertiary education

Many of the above considerations, of course, apply equally to the institutions of higher education. Indeed, it is in the area of tertiary education that the most dramatic developments of the next decade are likely to take place. A few years ago a tertiary education was a reality for only the privileged few. The more fortunate of these attended a degree course at a university, the less fortunate struggled as evening students along a tortuous path to a technical diploma. A few students, especially those with a sub-matriculation secondary education, attended teachers' colleges or agricultural colleges. The division between these educational institutions was clear cut; their functions and clientele were well defined; the university shone out like the sun itself, the peak of the educational pyramid.

Now, however, the whole question of higher education is in the melting pot. Amid a deplorable lack of advance planning, many tertiary institutions, with ill-defined goals, ill-defined functions, and an ill-defined clientele are eyeing one another with interest and even suspicion.

Much of the upheaval in higher education is officially regarded as the product of recommendations contained in the Martin Report, but already there are signs that the developments envisaged by the Martin Committee—whether acted upon by the Federal Government or not—are getting out of hand.

The Martin Committee recommended the establishment in each state of an institute of colleges, which would include most of the non-university tertiary institutions. One state, New South Wales, has decided not to establish such a body, but to set up a number of separate specialized institutes. These institutes were not seen initially as being degree granting, their emphasis being upon teaching and technical expertise rather than upon research. Already it is clear that the Victoria Institute of Colleges has broken new ground with the introduction of a degree course in pharmacy.[1]

The Martin Committee recommended the establishment in certain rural centres and in Canberra of Colleges of Advanced Education with status within the institutes. The Colleges of Advanced Education were seen as diploma granting institutions, and this understanding was such as to lead the states to believe that, initially, the salaries of personnel in the colleges would be of sub-university standard. The salaries of key officers of, for example, the Bathurst College of Advanced Education in New South Wales, have been advertised at that level. Meanwhile, an extraordinary decision was made in the national capital to advertise the salaries of the senior officers of the Canberra College of Advanced Education at *university* level.[2]

The Martin Committee recommended that the agricultural colleges, hitherto clearly sub-tertiary institutions, should upgrade their offerings to allow for matriculation entry and three or four year courses. In some states, notably Queensland, substantial progress has been made towards that end; in others, like Victoria, real progress seems a long way off. In New South Wales the future of the agricultural colleges seems unclear, to say the least.

The position of the teachers' colleges is even more uncertain, for neither the federal nor state governments appear, on the whole, to have taken seriously the Martin recommendations. Canberra did not accept in full the recommendation that federal funds should be made available for the support of teacher education, and with only one or two exceptions the state governments have done little to set up effectively the recommended Boards of Teacher Education. Of course, the Martin Committee's recommendations on teacher education were themselves remarkably short-sighted. In relegating the key figure in the educational process to a sub-university institution clearly separated from the main stream of academic study, especially in the social sciences, they performed a gross disservice to education generally and to Australian children in particular, but at least their recommendations contained *some* growing points. Much to the disappointment of teachers' associations, the only clear-cut development has been the decision to include teacher education in the programmes of the Colleges of Advanced Education at Bathurst and Canberra.

What might we see emerging from this most unholy mess during the next decade? We might reasonably expect the following:

1. A growing pressure from all types of newly established tertiary institutions to become chartered as degree granting bodies;
2. A growing pressure from these institutions for research funds comparable to those sought by university staff;
3. A growing recognition on the part of universities of the qualifications of these institutions for entry into both undergraduate and postgraduate programmes within the universities.

In other words, there are *already* clear signs that the new institutions will, like the United States institutes of technology and teachers' colleges and the British C.A.T.S. and teachers' colleges, move into the university area.

The position of the teachers' colleges will be especially interesting. Of all states, only New South Wales has still officially to espouse a policy of a three-year minimum period of training. We can reasonably assume that shortly the teachers' colleges of this state will adopt this minimum period of training of three years, but will follow different organizational paths: some as parts of Colleges of Advanced Education, some as Colleges of Education of adjoining universities, some as independent institutions in their own right, some perhaps as members of a collegial state university. Within a decade, therefore, we should see quite marked changes in teacher education. Most of these changes will be, in my view, second-best solutions, but they will almost certainly be for the better when compared with present practice.

How might all these changes affect the universities? Almost certainly they will hasten the moves within universities for the adoption of academic and organizational practices which are closer to the North American than to the traditional British pattern. Such moves are already well defined, e.g. course work for postgraduate degrees, multiple professorships in particular disciplines, permanent deanships, semester or trimester teaching units, graduate schools. The development of the new tertiary institutions as virtually undergraduate universities will almost certainly place much greater demands on the existing universities' postgraduate training resources. It is not too fanciful to suggest that by the 1980's one or two of our universities will, like their prestigious U.S. counterparts, have as many as one third of their students engaged in postgraduate work.

One of the more positive outcomes of all this development might well be a new interest in *teaching* at the tertiary level. It is already well known that the more technically and professionally oriented departments of universities are interested in teaching methods and aids, and it is to be hoped that the new institutions whose concern is, in theory at least, with teaching rather than research, will lead the way. In this regard it is reasonable to expect that some of the new institutions will develop special interests in the teaching of evening and external students.

Even a cursory perusal of likely developments must lead the protagonists of educational planning to throw their hats in the air, for national planning must come, and come quickly, if chaos, unnecessary competition, and waste are to be avoided. But who is to plan for the planners? Already the New South Wales tertiary institutions are subject to "visitation" by the

Australian Universities Commission, the Commonwealth Advisory Committee on Advanced Education and the New South Wales Universities Board. How long will it be before we boast a *New South Wales* Advisory Committee on Higher Education? Surely federal and state interests in higher education must be rationalized before a state of absurdity is reached.

Finally, all of the political realities referred to at the beginning of this paper will place great and profound pressures upon university education as we now know it. Should the long established universities fail to recognize and keep up with Australia's new political and economic role, there can be little doubt that governments, both federal and state, will establish universities of a somewhat different type which *will* meet the new demands. Some states may establish condominia on the United States pattern, in order to share in scarce specialized educational resources; others may request the Federal Government to recognize one or two institutions as regional or even national centres for teaching and research in given areas; others may urge the support or establishment of private or even church-owned universities. The position is, surely, that we are in the process of departing rapidly from the long established mediaeval tradition of the university as a monopoly-holder in advanced education. In observing the swing away from this concept we shall have to learn from the mistakes of our United States colleagues and exercise great vigilance, for while the educational world of tomorrow is not entirely controllable, we should at least attempt to ensure that that which is best in our university tradition remains untrammeled.

General

One of the most important and far-reaching developments in education during the next ten years or so almost certainly will be increased "democratization" in decision making regarding education, as traditional bureaucratic structures adapt to meet new social needs and as more and more educational administrators receive university training as administrators. Already most state school teachers' associations have earned considerable representation on appointments, promotion, and syllabus committees, while some are pressing for teachers to be given responsibilities affecting major policy making. The proposed New South Wales Education Commission, for example, would give teachers a substantial say in policy making, certainly on a much wider range of issues than the rather clumsy and restricted teachers' tribunals set up in Victoria and Western Australia in recent decades. Even if the New South Wales Education Commission does not become a reality, it is unlikely that teachers will cease their demands for a say in matters affecting their profession, and with the example of the National Teaching Council for Scotland to follow, who can blame them?

Whether or not our educational policy makers like the look of it, the fact is that teachers throughout the world are on the move, and are working through a combination of both professional and union procedures to have their voices heard in high places.

There can be little doubt that teachers in Australian non-government schools, too, will be seeking industrial agreements before long and will, perhaps, be seeking an increasing say in the government of their schools. The problem of their participation in decision making is just as great, if not greater, than for teachers in government schools, for the powers of bishops, provincials, and headmasters are no less for apparently having the angels on their side!

Indeed, the position of the non-government schools generally has reached a critical stage. It seems very likely that in the near future the Catholic schools of Australia, bedevilled by rising costs and teacher shortages, will become in fact, if not in name, merely another form of government school, lacking, in all probability, at least some of the distinctly religious flavour of the "public" Catholic schools of Alberta and Scotland.

The independent non-Catholic schools on the other hand, and especially those whose heads are members of the Headmasters' Conference, are likely to become rather more exclusivist than they are today, for the places they offer are unlikely to increase in anything like the same proportion as the increase in the population generally. While the general availability of government high schools and the improvement of transport services may well decrease proportionately the demand for places in such schools, there can be little doubt that they will remain at the end of the 1970's as a disproportionately high source of university matriculants, especially those interested in the "high" professions.

A fascinating question of concern to all Australians is the future of educational provision in the Australian Capital Territory. There seems little doubt that within the next decade a federal government will decide to constitute an independent educational system for the Territory. Such a move certainly *should* be in the interests of Australian education, for a system of the size of that proposed seems to be well suited to educational innovation and experimentation. The key question, of course, is what shape will the new organization take? Will it merely emulate New South Wales? Will it set up a board of education on the English or United States pattern? Will it provide for citizen participation in at least some aspects of school organization on perhaps the New Zealand pattern? Will it involve the non-government schools as part of the system? A wild guess suggests that the new system will indeed differ from that known to Australians up to the present, and such a move can hardly be denounced by those who are concerned about the extraordinary degree of centralization affecting educational decision making in this country.

Beyond Canberra, in the far-off states, some reorganization of educational structures will obviously be necessary during the next ten years. Already New South Wales has greatly extended its "area directorate" system, while similar moves are afoot in South Australia. Great care will need to be taken to ensure that such moves do not deteriorate into *re*centralization rather than *de*centralization. It does seem likely, if recent Victorian legislation provides a clue, that citizen participation in school government is likely to increase, though not in the strictly professional area. The growing power of the organized—and lobbying— activities of parents and citizens' groups makes such developments very likely, if only because their voices will be heard even louder as the general level of education in our society creeps higher and higher.

In conclusion, in view of the concern of this Conference, we might well ask: what of adult education and university extension generally during the next decade? All the signs of a pressing and urgent demand for such education are present. We are to lead in Asia and we know little about Asia. We are to trade with Japan and we know no Japanese. We are to be given much leisure and we do not know how to use leisure. We are worried about our primary industries and we have plenty of experts prepared to advise us on those industries.

Everything around us, then, suggests that we will need university extension as we have never needed it before. And yet I cannot be over-optimistic. So often during the last century have we heard the same arguments presented and so often have we been appalled at the tiny proportion of the population which has shown any interest in its assumed needs.

I do not suggest, of course, that university extension will march backwards—far from it—but I suspect that if we are not careful much of the growth in class enrolments will be disproportionately high in courses like ballet, sculpture, and pottery which are "cultural" pursuits rather than the utilitarian pursuits or the more academic "liberal" studies which our place in geography and history would seem to demand.

Even the strongest supporters of university extension cannot but be disturbed at the condition of adult education generally in Australia today. Adult educators are disappointed at the very small proportion of the population which buys their wares. They are still stunned at the recent "thumbs down" attitude adopted by the Australian Universities Commission. They are worried about their lack of academic standing when compared with their colleagues in other university departments and faculties. They are divided within themselves on questions of specialization and general interests, of techniques like so-called community development, of entrepreneurial and teaching roles.

These are all questions which need to be taken up by the adult educator during the next decade, and taken up they *must* be. Australia saw only too clearly earlier this century the effects on adult education of confusion in goals, undue diversification of interests, and internal strife. Is the time drawing near when departments of university extension should see themselves solely as entrepreneurs or administrators charged with the task of releasing the floodwaters of university learning into the populace?

Unless there is some fundamental reorientation and reorganization of adult education and extension very soon, its future looks bleak indeed. Will disciplined research into adult education and the professional training of adult educators provide some guidelines for future growth? The question of innovation and change in adult education faces many dragons in the path and no dragons are fiercer than the attitudes of some adult educators themselves.

CONCLUSION

The great questions facing Australian educators generally, and not the least adult educators, during the next decade are those of innovation and change, of the adaptation of educational structures and functions which are still nineteenth century in concept to those more applicable to the close-at-hand twenty-first century.

As Phillip Coombes of the International Institute for Educational Planning put the problem to the 1967 International Conference on the World Crisis in Education:

> There . . . has arisen a serious disfunction, a disparity taking many forms, between educational systems and their environment . . . What can the managers of educational systems do on their own? The one most vital thing they can do is to overcome their own inherent inertia in the face of a clear and immediate challenge to the relevance of their systems. No more than a grown man can wear the clothes that fitted him as a child can an educational system stand still and oppose making change while a world of things is on the move all around it . . .

Coombes's advice is equally a loud and clear call to all participating in this Conference. In a moment of truth he adds,

> It would pay imperfect homage to the truth to suggest that the teaching profession itself—viewed in the mass—is avid

for professional self-criticism, or is alive to opportunities for innovations that will help teachers achieve more in the classroom, where now they have little chance to think. Indeed, one must note an ironic fact about the worldwide educational crisis. It is that although the crisis has occurred amid a universal expansion of knowledge, education, as the prime creator and purveyor of knowledge, has generally failed to apply to its own inner life the function it performs in society at large ... Education thus places itself in an ambiguous moral position—it exhorts everyone else to mend his ways, yet seems stubbornly resistant to innovation in its own affairs.

If this is true—and Coombes has a habit of cutting close to the bone—then the next ten years presents us all with a challenge indeed. Whether through systems analysis, empirical research or good old-fashioned committee enquiry, we will need to accumulate and weigh up our data and plan for action. All decision making, including educational decision making, involves risks, and an unwillingness to take carefully calculated risks is not only immature and irrational, it is also a strong guarantee of lethargy, complacency and obsolescence.

NOTES TO TEXT

ONE: THE CHALLENGE OF EDUCATIONAL ADMINISTRATION

1. See W. G. Walker, "Educational Administration", in R. W. T. Cowan (ed.), *Education for Australians* (Melbourne: Cheshire, 1964), chap. 9.
2. Ordway Tead, *The Art of Administration* (New York: McGraw-Hill, 1951), p. 101.
3. *Ibid.*
4. *Ibid.*, p. 202.
5. J. Hemphill *et. al.*, *Dimensions of Administrative Performance* (New York: Teachers' College, Columbia University, 1961) (typescript).
6. H. A. Simon, *Administrative Behavior* (New York: Macmillan, 1957), p. xiv.
7. Francois Cillié, *Centralization or Decentralization?* (Contributions to Education, No. 789 [New York: Teachers' College, Columbia University, 1940]).
8. See A. W. Halpin, "A Paradigm for Research in Administrator Behavior", R. F. Campbell and R. T. Gregg, *Administrative Behavior in Education* (New York: Harper, 1957), p. 179.
9. K. S. Cunningham and W. C. Radford, *Training the Administrator* (Melbourne: Australian Council for Educational Research, 1963).
10. T. J. Jenson and D. L. Clark, *Educational Administration* (New York: Centre for Applied Research in Education, 1964), p. 106.
11. W. G. Walker, "The Fly Catchers", chap. 10 this volume.
12. M. E. Dimock, *The Executive in Action* (New York: Harper, 1945).
13. I. Kandel, *Types of Administration* (Melbourne: Australian Council for Educational Research, 1938).
14. R. G. Barker and P. V. Gump, *Big School, Small School* (Stanford, California: Stanford University Press, 1964), pp. 194-202.
15. W. G. Walker, "Theory and Practice in Educational Administration", Chapter 7 this volume.
16. K. M. Dallenbach, quoted by D. E. Griffiths, "Towards a Theory of Administrative Behavior", in Campbell and Gregg, *op. cit.*, p. 366.
17. J. W. Getzels, "Theory and Practice in Educational Administration: An Old Question Revisited", in R. F. Campbell and J. M. Lipham, *Administrative Theory as a Guide to Action* (Chicago: Midwest Administration Center, 1960), p. 41. (See also Chapter 7, this volume.)
18. George E. Miller, "The Professorship in Medicine", in Donald J. Willower and Jack Culbertson (eds.), *The Professorship in Educational Administration* (Columbus, Ohio: University Council for Educational Administration, 1964), pp. 74-75.

two: PROBLEMS OF SCHOOL ORGANIZATION

1. P. W. Joyce, *A Handbook of School Management* (Dublin: McGlashan and Gill, 1867).
2. *Ibid.*, p. 25.
3. *Ibid.*, p. 30.
4. See J. W. Getzels, "Theory and Practice in Educational Administration: An Old Question Revisited", in R. F. Campbell and J. M. Lipham, *Administrative Theory as a Guide to Action* (Chicago: Midwest Administration Center, 1960). Also see Chapter 7 this volume.
5. Ordway Tead, *The Art of Administration* (New York: McGraw-Hill, 1951).
6. F. G. Cornell and J. Inabnit, "Administrative Organization as Social Structure", *Progressive Education*, vol. XXX, no. 2 (November 1952).
7. R. C. Lonsdale, "Maintaining the Organization in Dynamic Equilibrium", (Chap. 7), in D. E. Griffiths (ed.), *Behavioral Science and Educational Administration* (Chicago: National Society for the Study of Education, 1964).
8. Cornell and Inabnit, *op. cit.*
9. *Ibid.*
10. J. Dewey, *Human Nature and Conduct* (New York: Holt, 1922), p. 306.
11. J. A. Culbertson, "The Preparation of Administrators", in D. E. Griffiths, *op. cit.*, chap. 14.
12. C. I. Barnard, *The Functions of the Executive* (Cambridge, Mass.: Harvard University Press, 1938), p. 286.
13. Lonsdale, *op. cit.*, p. 173.
14. See, for example, G. W. Bassett, A. R. Crane, and W. G. Walker, *Headmasters for Better Schools* (St. Lucia: University of Queensland Press, 1963).
15. A. G. Hughes, *Education and the Democratic Ideal* (London: Longmans, 1951).
16. K. Wiles, *Supervision for Better Schools* (Englewood Cliffs, N.J.: Prentice Hall, 1957).
17. R. Bierstedt, *The Social Order* (New York: McGraw-Hill, 1957), p. 286.
18. R. T. Gregg, "The Administrative Process", in R. F. Campbell and R. T. Gregg, *Administrative Behavior in Education* (New York: Harper, 1962), chap. 8, p. 67.
19. S. G. Knezevich, *Administration of Public Education* (New York: Harper, 1962), p. 67.
20. L. A. Urwick, *The Elements of Administration* (London: Pitman, 1961), p. 53.
21. Knezevich, *op cit.*, p. 68.
22. E. G. Guba, "Research in Internal Administration: What Do We Know?" in Campbell and Lipham, *op. cit.*

23. J. W. Getzels, "Administration as a Social Process", in A. W. Halpin, *Administrative Theory in Education* (Chicago: Midwest Administration Center, 1958).

24. M. E. Dimock, *The Executive in Action* (New York: Harper, 1945).

25. T. J. Jenson and D. L. Clarke, *Educational Administration* (New York: Center for Applied Research in Education, 1964), p. 52.

26. R. M. Stogdill, *Individual Behaviour and Group Achievement*: *A Theory* (New York: Oxford University Press, 1959).

THREE: TRAINING THE EDUCATIONAL
ADMINISTRATOR

1. See, e.g., American Association of School Administrators, *Inservice Education for School Administration* (Washington, D.C.: 1963), p. 22.

2. K. S. Cunningham and W. C. Radford, *Training the Administrator* (Melbourne: Australian Council for Educational Research, 1963).

3. L. F. Urwick, *The Elements of Administration* (London: Pitman, 1961).

4. L. F. Urwick, "Management", *Current Affairs Bulletin*, vol. XXX, no. 8 (Sydney, 1962).

5. J. A. Culbertson, "The Preparation of Administrators", in *Behavioral Science and Educational Administration*, Sixty-third Yearbook (Chicago: National Society for the Study of Education, 1964), chap. 14.

6. Frederick Taylor, *The Principles of Scientific Management* (New York: Harper, 1911).

7. E. P. Cubberley, *Public School Administration* (Boston: Houghton Mifflin, 1916).

8. E. Mayo, *The Social Problems of an Industrial Civilization* (Cambridge Mass.: Harvard University Press, 1945).

9. Culbertson, *op. cit.*, p. 305.

10. G. W. Bassett, A. R. Crane, and W. G. Walker, *Headmasters for Better Schools* (2nd. ed.; St. Lucia: University of Queensland Press, 1967).

11. H. A. Simon, *Administrative Behavior* (New York: Macmillan, 1947).

12. C. I. Barnard, *The Functions of the Executive* (Cambridge, Mass.: Harvard University Press, 1938).

13. A. W. Halpin, *Administrative Theory in Education* (Chicago: Midwest Administration Center, 1958).

14. D. E. Griffiths, *Administrative Theory* (New York: Appleton, 1959).

15. R. F. Campbell and R. T. Gregg, *Administrative Behavior in Education* (New York: Harper, 1957).

16. Dwight Waldo, quoted by Culbertson, *op. cit.*, p. 307.

17. Culbertson, *op. cit.*, p. 316.

18. See D. E. Griffiths, "The Case Method of Teaching Educational Administration: A Reappraisal 1963", in *Journal of Educational Administration*, vol. 1, no. 11 (October 1963).

19. C. G. Sargent, and E. L. Belisle, *Educational Administration*: *Cases and Concepts* (Boston: Houghton Mifflin, 1955).

20. J. A. Culbertson, P. B. Jacobsen, and T. L. Reller, *Administrative Relationships* (Englewood Cliffs, N.J.: Prentice-Hall, 1960).
21. *Instructional Materials, 1964* (University Council for Educational Administration, 65 South Oval Drive, Columbus 10, Ohio) (*gratis*).
22. W. G. Walker (ed.), *The Principal at Work: Case Studies in School Administration* (2nd ed.; St. Lucia: University of Queensland Press, 1968).
23. See J. K. Hemphill *et. al.*, *Administrative Performance and Personality* (New York: Columbia Teachers' College, 1962).
24. Charles Gregg, quoted by J. A. Culbertson, *et. al.*, in *Administrative Relationships, op. cit.*, p. 74.
25. T. P. Nunn, *Education: Its Data and First Principles* (London: Arnold, 1920).
26. W. G. Walker, "Educational Administration", in R. W. T. Cowan (ed.), *Education for Australians* (Melbourne: Cheshire 1964), chap. 9, p. 195.
27. A. W. Halpin, "Ways of Knowing", in R. F. Campbell and J. M. Lipham, *Administrative Theory as a Guide to Action* (Chicago: Midwest Administration Center, 1960), chap. 1, p. 14.

FOUR: THE ADMINISTRATIVE REVOLUTION:
THE ROLE OF THE UNIVERSITY

1. For a fuller discussion of this point, see R. F. Campbell, J. E. Corbally, and J. A. Ramseyer, *Introduction to Educational Administration* (Boston: Allyn and Bacon, 1962), pp. 8off.
2. See W. G. Sumner, *Folkways* (Boston: Ginn, 1911).
3. *Curriculum and Examinations in Secondary Schools* (London: H.M.S.O., 1943).
4. *General Education in a Free Society* (Cambridge, Mass.: Harvard University Press, 1945).
5. *Report of the Committee Appointed to Survey Secondary Education in New South Wales* (Sydney: Government Printer, 1958).
6. See G. W. Bassett, "The Characteristics of a Good School", in *Conference on School Administration* (St. Lucia, University of Queensland, 1961).
7. See W. G. Walker, "The Springtown Red", *External Studies Gazette*, vol. VI, no. 5 (July 1962).
8 F. W. Taylor, *Scientific Management* (New York: Harper, 1947) (contains several of Taylor's works).
9. Henri Fayol, *General and Industrial Management* (London: Pitman, 1949).
10. H. C. Metcalf and L. Urwick (eds.), *Dynamic Administration: The Collected Papers of Mary Parker Follett* (London: Pitman, 1957).
11. Elton Mayo, *The Human Problems of an Industrial Civilization* (Boston: Harvard University Press, 1946). See also J. A. C. Brown, *The Social Psychology of Industry* (Harmondsworth: Penguin, 1956).
12. C. I. Barnard, *The Functions of the Executive* (Cambridge, Mass.: Harvard University Press, 1938).

13. One important product of this venture is: R. F. Campbell and R. T. Gregg (eds.), *Administrative Behavior in Education* (New York: Harper, 1957).

14. See W. G. Walker, "The Canadian Educational Association Project in Educational Leadership", *Australian Journal of Education*, vol. III, no. 2 (July 1959).

15. See, e.g., "The Leader Behaviour and Leadership Ideology of Educational Administrators and Aircraft Commanders", *Harvard Educational Review*, XXV, no. 1 (Winter 1955), pp. 18-32.

16. See O. Tead, *The Art of Administration* (New York: McGraw-Hill, 1951), and F. Hooper, *Management Survey* (Hammondsworth: Penguin, 1960).

17. See Michael Young, *The Rise of the Meritocracy* (Harmondsworth: Penguin, 1961), pp. 79ff.

18. See I. Kandel, *Types of Administration* (Melbourne: Australian Council for Educational Research, 1961), and R. F. Butts, *Assumptions Underlying Australian Education* (Melbourne: Australian Council for Educational Research, 1955).

19. See F. S. Cillié, *Centralization or Decentralization?* ("Contributions to Education", No. 789 [New York: Teachers' College, Columbia University, 1940]).

20. G. W. Bassett (ed.), *Conference on School Administration* (St. Lucia: University of Queensland, 1961).

21. O. R. Jones (ed.), *The School Principal* (Melbourne: Cheshire, 1962).

22. G. W. Bassett, A. R. Crane, and W. G. Walker, *Headmasters for Better Schools* (2nd ed.; St. Lucia: University of Queensland Press, 1967).

23. Ortega y Gasset, *Mission of the University* (London: Kegan Paul, 1946).

24. L. F. Urwick, "Management", *Current Affairs Bulletin*, vol. XXX, no. 8 (Sydney, 1962).

25. D. E. Griffiths, *Administrative Theory* (New York: Appleton-Century-Crofts, 1959).

26. Talcott Parsons, "Some Ingredients of a General Theory of Formal Organization", in A. W. Halpin (ed.), *Administrative Theory in Education* (Chicago: Midwest Administration Center, 1958).

27. A. P. Coladarci and J. W. Getzels, *The Use of Theory in Educational Administration* (Stanford, Calif.: Stanford University Press, 1955).

28. W. H. Lucio and J. D. McNeil, *Supervision: A Synthesis of Thought and Action* (New York: McGraw-Hill, 1962).

29. Albert Einstein and L. Infeld, *The Evolution of Physics* (New York: Simon and Shuster, 1938), p. 33.

FIVE: DIPLOMA IN EDUCATIONAL ADMINISTRATION
OF THE UNIVERSITY OF NEW ENGLAND

1. "Teaching and Research in Educational Administration", *Journal of Educational Administration*, vol. II, no. 1 (1964); and "Educational

Administration" in R. T. Cowan (ed.), *Education for Australians* (Melbourne: Cheshire, 1964).

2. "The Administrative Revolution: The Role of the University in the Development of the School as an Educative Community", *Australian Journal of Higher Education*, vol. II, no. 1 (1962).

3. "The Canadian Education Association Project in Educational Leadership", in *Australian Journal of Education*, vol. III, no. 2 (1959); and "What the School Administrator Can Learn from Administrators Outside the Education System" and "Policy Making Within the School", *Conference on School Administration* (St. Lucia: University of Queensland, 1961).

4. "Theory and Practice in School Administration", *Conference on School Administration* (St. Lucia: University of Queensland, 1964).

5. K. S. Cunningham and W. C. Radford, *Training the Administrator* (Melbourne, Australian Council for Educational Research, 1963).

6. With G. W. Bassett and A. R. Crane, *Headmasters for Better Schools* (2nd ed.; St. Lucia: University of Queensland Press, 1967).

7. *The Principal at Work: Case Studies in School Administration* (2nd ed.; St. Lucia: University of Queensland Press, 1968).

SIX: TEACHING AND RESEARCH IN EDUCATIONAL ADMINISTRATION

1. H. A. Simon *et al.*, *Public Administration* (New York: Knopf, 1950), p. 6.

2. J. G. Cannon, *Comments on Education in U.S.A. and Victoria* (Melbourne: Australia Council for Educational Research, 1932).

3. K. A. Cunningham and G. E. Phillips, *Some Aspects of Education in the United States* (Melbourne: Australian Council for Educational Research, 1930).

4. J. F. Cramer, *Australian Schools Through American Eyes* (Melbourne: Australian Council for Educational Research, 1936).

5. I. L. Kandel, *Types of Administration* (Melbourne: Australian Council for Educational Research, 1961).

6. C. R. McRae, *An Australian Looks at American Schools* (Melbourne: Australian Council for Educational Research, 1939).

7. R. F. Butts, *Assumptions Underlying Australian Education* (Melbourne: Australian Council for Educational Research, 1955).

8. J. W. Tibble, Reflections on Australian Education, in *New Horizons in Education*, XVIII (Summer 1957-58), pp. 41-43.

9. R. W. B. Jackson, *Emergent Needs in Australian Education* (Toronto: Department of Educational Research, 1961).

10. Cramer, *op. cit.*, p. 19.

11. Cunningham and Phillips, *op. cit.*, p. 22.

12. W. G. Walker, *Report to the Carnegie Corporation of New York* (1959) (typescript).

13. W. G. Walker, "Training the Educational Administrator", chap. 3 this volume.

14. R. F. Campbell, "What Peculiarities in Educational Administration Make It a Special Case?" in A. W. Halpin (ed.), *Administrative Theory in Education* (Chicago: Midwest Administration Center, 1958).

15. R. N. Bush, "The Teacher-Pupil Relationship in Australian Secondary Schools", *Australian Journal of Education*, vol. II, no. 1 (1958).

16. O. B. Graff and C. M. Street, "Developing a Value Framework for Educational Administration", in R. F. Campbell and R. T. Gregg, (eds.), *Administrative Behavior in Education* (New York: Harper, 1957).

17. See, e.g., A. W. Halpin, "The Leader Behavior and Leadership Ideology of Educational Administrators and Aircraft Commanders", in *Harvard Educational Review*, vol. XXV (Winter 1955), pp. 18-32.

18. See W. G. Walker, *Future Occupational Plans of a Sample of Beginning Teachers* (typescript).

19. *Judging Schools with Wisdom*, (Washington, D.C.: American Association of School Administrators, 1959), p. 4.

20. P. R. Mort and F. G. Cornell, *A Guide for Self-Appraisal* (New York: Teachers' College, Columbia University, 1937).

21. P. R. Mort *et al. The Growing Edge: An Instrument for Measuring the Adaptability of School Systems* (New York: Teachers' College, Columbia University, 1946).

22. Halpin, *op. cit.*

23. A. W. Halpin, "A Paradigm for Research in Administrator Behavior", in R. F. Campbell and R. T. Gregg (eds.), *Administrative Behavior in Education* (New York: Harper, 1957), p. 159.

24. D. E. Griffiths, "Administration as Decision Making", in A. W. Halpin (ed.), *Administrative Theory in Education* (Chicago: Midwest Administration Center, 1958), p. 127.

25. *Inservice Education for School Administration* (Washington, D.C.: American Association of School Administrators, 1963), p. 22.

26. H. A. Simon, *Administrative Behavior* (New York: Macmillan, 1957), p. xiv.

SEVEN: THEORY AND PRACTICE IN EDUCATIONAL ADMINISTRATION

1. R. Boyd, *The Australian Ugliness* (Melbourne: Penguin, 1963).

2. Ordway Tead, *The Art of Administration* (New York: McGraw-Hill, 1951).

3. R. F. Campbell and R. T. Gregg, *Administrative Behavior in Education* (New York: Harper, 1957).
   R. F. Campbell and J. M. Lipham, *Administrative Theory as a Guide to Action* (Chicago: Midwest Administration Center, 1960).
   A. P. Coladarci and J. W. Getzels, *The Use of Theory in Educational Administration* (Stanford, Calif.: Stanford University Press, 1955).

D. E. Griffiths, *Administrative Theory* (New York: Appleton-Century-Crofts, 1959).

A. W. Halpin, *Administrative Theory in Education* (Chicago: Midwest Administration Center, 1958).

Behavioral Science and Educational Administration, Sixty-third Yearbook (Chicago: National Society for the Study of Education, 1964).

4. D. E. Griffiths, "The Nature and Meaning of Theory", in *Behavioral Science and Educational Administration*, Sixty-third Yearbook (Chicago: National Society for the Study of Education, 1964), p. 98.

5. J. D. Thompson, "Modern Approaches to Theory in Administration", in Halpin, *op. cit.*, p. 21.

6. Griffiths, *Administrative Theory*, pp. 13-19.

7. D. E. Griffiths, "Toward a Theory of Administrative Behavior", in Campbell and Gregg, *op. cit.*, p. 360.

8. W. Johnson, *People in Quandaries* (New York: Harper, 1946), quoted by Griffiths.

9. H. A. Simon, *Administrative Behavior* (New York: Macmillan, 1947, p. 37).

10. Griffiths, in Campbell and Gregg, *op. cit.*, p. 363.

11. K. M. Dallenbach, "The Place of Theory in Science", quoted by Griffiths, *Administrative Theory*, p. 366.

12. S. P. Marland, "Superintendents' Concerns About Research Applications in Educational Administration", in Campbell and Lipham, *op. cit.*, p. 23.

13. J. W. Getzels, "Theory and Practice in Educational Administration: An Old Question Revisited", in Campbell and Lipham, *op. cit.*, p. 41.

14. *Ibid.*, p. 42.

15. G. C. Homans, *The Human Group* (New York: Harcourt, 1950), pp. 16-17.

16. Griffiths, *op. cit.*, p. 363-64.

17. A. W. Halpin, "Ways of Knowing", in Campbell and Lipham, *op. cit.*, p. 3.

18. Getzels, *op. cit.*, p. 38.

19. H. Fayol, *General and Industrial Administration* (London, 1919).

20. L. F. Urwick, *The Elements of Administration* (London: Pitman, 1961).

21. H. C. Metcalfe and L. Urwick (eds.), *Dynamic Administration: The Collected Papers of Mary Parker Follett* (London: Pitman, 1957).

22. L. Gulick, "Notes on the Theory of Organization", in L. Gulick and L. Urwick, *Papers on the Science of Administration* (New York: Columbia University, 1937).

23. Tead, *op. cit.*

24. E. Mayo, *The Social Problems of an Industrial Civilization* (Cambridge, Mass., Harvard University Press, 1945).

25. C. I. Barnard, *The Functions of the Executive* (Cambridge, Mass.: Harvard University Press, 1938).

26. Simon, *op. cit.*
27. Chris Argyris, "The Individual in Organization: An Empirical Test", in *Administrative Science Quarterly*, vol. IV, no. 2 (September 1959), pp. 145-67.
28. D. E. Griffiths, "Administration as Decision Making", in Halpin, *Administrative Theory in Education.*
29. J. K. Hemphill, "Administration as Problem Solving", in Halpin, *Administrative Theory in Education.*
30. E. G. Guba, "Research in Internal Administration: What Do We Know?", in Campbell and Lipham, *op. cit.*
31. J. W. Getzels, "Administration as a Social Process", in Halpin, *Administration Theory in Education.*
32. Griffiths, "The Nature and Meaning of Theory".
33. Hemphill, *et al., Administrative Performance and Personality* (New York: Columbia, 1962).
34. Jack Culbertson, "U.C.E.A.: Its Program and Prospects", in *Journal of Educational Administration*, vol. II, no. 2 (October 1964), pp. 80-93.
35. A. W. Halpin, "A Paradigm for Research in Administrator Behavior", in Campbell and Gregg, *op. cit.*
36. Getzels, "Theory and Practice in Educational Administration: An Old Question Revisited", in Campbell and Lipham, *op. cit.*
37. Guba, *op. cit.*
38. *Ibid.*, p. 126.
39. Griffiths, "Toward a Theory of Administrative Behavior".

EIGHT: DECISION MAKING IN AUSTRALIAN EDUCATIONAL SYSTEMS: CRITICS AND CONCEPTS

1. J. G. March and H. A. Simon, *Organizations* (New York: Wiley, 1958).
2. Floyd Hunter, *Community Power Structure: A Study of Decision-Making* (Chapel Hill, N.C.: University of North Carolina Press, 1953).
3. Roland Pellegrin, *Community Power Structure and Educational Decision-Making in the Local Community* (Eugene, Oregon: Center for the Advanced Study of Educational Administration, 1965) (mimeo), p. 3.
4. F. J. Willett, "Organization Theory: A Personal Review", *Journal of Educational Administration*, vol. II, no. 1 (May 1964), pp. 44-52.
5. D. E. Griffiths (ed.), *Behavioral Science and Educational Administration*, Sixty-third Yearbook, II (Chicago: National Society for the Study of Education, 1964).
6. Alonzo G. Grace (ed.), *Changing Conceptions in Educational Administration*, Forty-fifth Yearbook, II (Chicago: National Society for the Study of Education, 1964).
7. J. J. Schwab, "The Professorship in Educational Administration: Theory—Art—Practice", in D. J. Willower and Jack Culbertson (eds.), *The Professorship in Educational Administration*, (Columbus, Ohio: University Council for Educational Administration, 1964), chap. 4.

8. *Ibid.*, pp. 54-55.
9. D. J. Willower, "The Professorship in Educational Administration: A Rationale", in *The Professorship in Educational Administration*, chap. 6, p. 100.
10. R. T. Gregg, "Essay Preview of D. E. Griffiths (ed.), *Behavioral Science and Educational Administration*", in *Educational Administration Quarterly*, vol. I, no. 1 (Winter 1965), p. 46.
11. C. I. Barnard, *The Functions of the Executive* (Cambridge, Mass.: Harvard University Press, 1938).
12. Herbert A. Simon, *Administrative Behavior: A Study of Decision-Making Processes in Administrative Organization* (New York: Macmillan, 1957).
13. D. E. Griffiths, *Administrative Theory* (New York: Appleton-Century-Crofts, 1959).
14. W. R. Dill, "Decision-Making" (Chap. 9) in Griffiths (ed.), *Sixty-third Yearbook*, p. 220.
15. Robert Presthus, *The Organizational Society* (New York: Knopf, 1962).
16. Chris Argyris, *Personality and Organization: The Conflict Between the System and the Individual* (New York: Harper, 1957).
17. J. Meeker, G. H. Shure and M. S. Rogers, "A Research Approach to Complex Decision-Making", in J. A. Culbertson and S. P. Hencley (eds.), *Educational Research: New Perspectives* (Danville, Ill.: Interstate, 1963), chap. 11.
18. J. L. Kandel, *Types of Administration* (Melbourne: Australian Council for Educational Research, 1938), p. 51.
19. R. F. Butts, *Assumptions Underlying Australian Education* (Melbourne, Australian Council for Educational Research, 1955), p. 13.
20. R. W. B. Jackson, *Emergent Needs in Australian Education* (Toronto: University of Toronto Department of Educational Research, 1961), p. 25.
21. *Compulsory Education in Australia* (Paris: UNESCO, 1951).
22. Talcott Parsons, "Some Ingredients of a General Theory of Formal Organization", in A. W. Halpin (ed.), *Administrative Theory in Education* (Chicago: Midwest Administration Center, 1958), chap. 3.
23. R. W. B. Jackson, *op. cit.*, p. 5.
24. R. F. Butts, *op. cit.*, p. 13.
25. D. E. Griffiths, "The Nature and Meaning of Theory", in Griffiths (ed.), Sixty-Third Yearbook. Griffiths relies heavily on Gordon Hearn, *Theory Building in Social Work* (Toronto: University of Toronto Press, 1958), chap. 5.
26. Robert Presthus, *op. cit.*
27. H. S. Sullivan, "Tensions, Interpersonal and International", in H. Cantrill (ed.), *Tensions That Cause Wars* (Urbana: University of Illinois Press, 1950).
28. Max Weber, as interpreted by Griffiths, "The Nature and Meaning of Theory".

29. Robert Presthus, *op. cit.*, p. 34.
30. D. E. Griffiths, *op. cit.*, p. 116.
31. James Hemming, "Urgent Case for Drastic Australian Educational Reform", in *New Horizons in Education*, no. 41 (Autumn 1950), p. 36.
32. R. N. Bush, "The Teacher-Pupil Relationship in Australian Secondary Schools", *Australian Journal of Education*, vol. II, no. 1 (April 1958), p. 41.
33. J. W. Getzels, "Theory and Practice in Educational Administration: An Old Question Revisited", in R. F. Campbell and J. M. Lipham, *Administrative Theory as a Guide to Action* (Chicago: Midwest Administration Center, 1960).
34. J. K. Hemphill *et al.*, *Administrative Performance and Personality* (New York: Columbia, 1962).
35. James Hemming, *op. cit.*, p. 38.
36. J. L. Kandel, *op. cit.*, p. 52.
37. R. F. Butts, *op. cit.*, p. 49.
38. A. W. Halpin and D. F. Croft, *The Organizational Climate of Schools* Chicago: Midwest Administration Center, 1963).

NINE: ORGANIZING THE SCHOOL FOR INDIVIDUAL DIFFERENCES: THE INNOVATIVE ROLE OF THE NON-GOVERNMENT SCHOOL

1. H. Benjamin, *The Saber-tooth Curriculum* (New York: McGraw-Hill, 1939).
2. N. L. Gage, *Handbook of Research on Teaching* (Chicago: Rand McNally, 1963).
3. B. O. Smith, "Conditions of Learning", in F. L. Morphett and C. O. Ryan (eds.), *Implications for Education of Prospective Changes in Society* (Designing Education for the Future Project, 1362 Lincoln Street, Denver, Colorado, 80203, U.S.A., January 1967), chap. 4.
4. *Individualizing Instruction* (Chicago: National Society for the Study of Education, 1962).
5. G. W. Bassett (ed.), *Each One is Different* (Melbourne: Australian Council for Educational Research, 1964).
6. J. L. Trump, and Dorsey Baynham, *Focus on Change: Guide to Better Schools* (Chicago: Rand McNally, 1961).
7. Robert H. Anderson, *Teaching in a World of Change* (New York: Harcourt, Brace and World, 1966).
8 D. W. Allen and D. E. Lay, *Flexible Scheduling. A Reality.* (Stanford University, California, 1966)(mimeo).
9. Theodore Brameld, *Education as Power* (New York: Holt, Rinehart and Winston, 1965).
10. Matthew B. Miles (ed.), *Innovation in Education* (New York: Teachers' College, Columbia University, 1964).
11. Richard O. Carlson, *Adoption of Educational Innovations* (Eugene: Oregon, Center for the Advanced Study of Educational Administration, 1965).

12. D. L. Clark and E. G. Guba, *An Examination of Potential Change Roles in Education* (Seminar on Innovation in Planning School Curricula, 1965) (typescript).

TWELVE: AUSTRALIAN EDUCATION: THE NEXT TEN YEARS

1. In 1969 the Federal Government accepted the recommendations of the Wiltshire Committee that Colleges of Advanced Education might be degree-granting through a national accrediting committee.

2. The Sweeney Report recommended that under certain conditions staff in Colleges of Advanced Education might be paid at University rates. This recommendation was accepted by the Federal Government in 1969.

INDEX TO PROPER NAMES

INDEX

BELMONT COLLEGE LIBRARY

INDEX